Power Verbs
for
Presenters

Power Verbs for Presenters

for

Presenters

HUNDREDS OF VERBS AND PHRASES TO PUMP UP YOUR SPEECHES AND PRESENTATIONS

MICHAEL LAWRENCE FAULKNER
WITH MICHELLE FAULKNER-LUNSFORD

Vice President, Publisher: Tim Moore
Associate Publisher and Director of Marketing: Amy Neidlinger
Executive Editor: Jeanne Glasser Levine
Editorial Assistant: Pamela Boland
Operations Specialist: Jodi Kemper
Marketing Manager: Megan Graue
Cover Designer: Chuti Prasertsith
Managing Editor: Kristy Hart
Project Editor: Anne Goebel
Copy Editor: Krista Hansing Editorial Services, Inc.
Proofreader: Chuck Hutchinson
Senior Indexer: Cheryl Lenser
Senior Compositor: Gloria Schurick
Manufacturing Buyer: Dan Uhrig

© 2013 by Michael Lawrence Faulkner

Publishing as FT Press

Upper Saddle River, New Jersey 07458

FT Press offers excellent discounts on this book when ordered in quantity for bulk purchases or special sales. For more information, please contact U.S. Corporate and Government Sales, 1-800-382-3419, corpsales@pearsontechgroup.com. For sales outside the U.S., please contact International Sales at international@pearsoned.com.

Company and product names mentioned herein are the trademarks or registered trademarks of their respective owners.

Printed in the United States of America

First Printing February 2013

ISBN-10: 0-13-315864-0
ISBN-13: 978-0-13-315864-9

Pearson Education LTD.
Pearson Education Australia PTY, Limited
Pearson Education Singapore, Pte. Ltd.
Pearson Education Asia, Ltd.
Pearson Education Canada, Ltd.
Pearson Educación de Mexico, S.A. de C.V.
Pearson Education—Japan
Pearson Education Malaysia, Pte. Ltd.

Library of Congress Cataloging-in-Publication Data

Faulkner, Michael.
   Power verbs for presenters : hundreds of verbs and phrases to pump up your speeches and presentations / Michael Faulkner, Michelle Faulkner-Lunsford. — 1 Edition.
      pages cm
   ISBN 978-0-13-315864-9 (pbk. : alk. paper) — ISBN 0-13-315864-0 (pbk. : alk. paper)
   1. Business presentations. 2. Public speaking. 3. English language—Verb. I. Faulkner-Lunsford, Michelle. II. Title.
   HF5718.22.F38 2013
   808.5'1—dc23
                          2012050098

Dedicated to my wife, Jo-Ann

She has been patient, inspirational, understanding, thoughtful, and loving beyond all expectations.

She is the ultimate power verb.

Table of Contents

Acknowledgments

Many people assisted with this book in many ways. Much of this help was a family affair. My wife, Jo-Ann, lent her love, patience, support, and advice. My son, Kenny, provided ideas for format when I was at a dead end. My grandsons, Andrew and Alex, looked up some words, and my daughter, Michelle, did yeoman's work, editing, writing content, working on style, and offering advice. Lastly, I want to acknowledge my peers, friends, and associates at DeVry University and Keller Graduate School of Management who inspire me, challenge me, and keep me on my toes.

About the Authors

Dr. Michael Lawrence Faulkner is the author of six books. He is a professor at the Keller Graduate School of Management at DeVry University. He is a former U.S. Marine, who spent 30 years in a variety of leadership and executive management positions with Fortune 500 firms and major nonprofit trade associations, as well as helping run the family business before beginning his second career in academics. Michael is a member of MENSA, a Rotary International Fellow, the Keller Master Teacher Award, and holds a Silver Certification by the Toastmaster's International. In addition to his Ph.D., Michael has earned two master's degrees, one from NYU and an MBA from NYIT.

Michelle Faulkner-Lunsford is a 2001 graduate of Middle Tennessee State University where she majored in English and minored in Writing. Mrs. Lunsford spent 10+ years in the world of advertising and marketing as an Account Manager and Director of Marketing and New Business Development, managing multi-million dollar accounts from male enhancement medications to beer ads. In 2011, Michelle left the corporate world for the opportunity to raise her daughter.

1

Why and How Power Verbs Can Pump Up Your Speeches and Presentations

Although no sources can trace it to him, an oft-used quotation is frequently attributed to Plutarch: "When Cicero spoke, people said, 'How well Cicero speaks!' But when Demosthenes spoke, they said, 'Let us march against Philip.'" The point is, the purpose of public speaking is usually—but not always—to persuade. As Rudyard Kipling said, "Words are the most powerful drug used by mankind." So whenever we speak, we are using a powerful device. Thomas Fuller might have said it best: "When the heart is afire, some sparks will fly out of the mouth." This book gives you some sparks.

This is not a style book. Nor is it a book on public speaking, per se. If that is what you are looking for, you can put this book down—but not too fast. You might want to read a little further; it might be just what you are looking for.

In this book, you will not learn specific skills of public speaking, oration, or rhetoric—or even how to deliver a good presentation. You will not learn in depth the skills of visualizing; managing stage fright; channeling your message; adapting to your audience; maintaining eye contact; using tone, cadence, and pitch; breathing properly; using hand gestures; selecting a topic; or handling questions. This book will make you a more powerful communicator because it helps you choose powerful verbs—the spark of sentences that people will remember. Power verbs are the flame that make your phrases and sentences ignite people's passions. Power verbs are the kindling that illuminates purpose and makes people want to take action … to march on Philip.

Why verbs, you might be asking? Not just verbs, but power verbs. First, more books have been written on language skills and verbs than you can imagine, and the world does not need another one of those books. Second, it would not be much fun to write or read another boring language skills book. If those books were so interesting, wouldn't there be a movie about one of them by now? Finally, this isn't a book about the old standby verbs. Everyone knows the 16 basic English language verbs: *be, do, have, come, go, see, seem, give, take, keep, make, put, send, say, let, get.*

Power verbs are emotionally edgy and powerfully positioned, with punch and pizzazz. Hundreds of books, guides, blogs, and more can help people learn how to put a speech together. Numerous guidebooks walk through writing and delivering a speech. However, in my 35 years of experience in giving hundreds of speeches and presentations, I've learned one fundamental truth: The power of the words selected and way they are delivered—the rhythm—make the greatest difference in the success of the presentation.

So why not write one book with every piece of advice, technique, and approach available? Simple: a fundamental principle called Pareto's Law, or the 80/20 principle. Simply stated, this widely accepted principle posits that the vast majority (the 80 percent) of all explanations for things such as solutions to problems and answers to questions are usually found in the smallest number of options (the 20 percent). So 80 percent of a great presentation or speech is in the 20 percent category for the proper words chosen and the rhythm in which they are delivered. As Dr. Frank Luntz says, "It's not what you say—it's what people hear" (Luntz, 2007, p. xi). Your audience translates your message through a prism of their own biases, interests, knowledge, awareness, feelings, attention span, and many other interpretative filters. Once you have spoken words, they no longer are yours. Other people will translate them, evaluate them, and measure them. Choose your words carefully—make them appropriate for the situation, and be aware of the power of words.

Poorly chosen words or speech used for hubris or evil can impact self-esteem, destroy morale, kill enthusiasm, inflame bias, incite hatred, lower expectations, and hold people back. Experts are learning more about the connection between words and people's human spirit and health. We've known for some time that insults and verbal harassment can make us physically and mentally ill. Inappropriate words can make work and home toxic, abusive environments. Empirical studies show that people who live or work in toxic environments suffer more colds, flu, heart attacks, depression—more of almost all chronic physical and emotional disorders than people who report living or working in happy, enjoyable, caring environments.

Hiding almost in plain sight for years, and now clearly recognized, is the connection between physical violence and words. Rarely does physical violence occur without some sort of verbal preamble. The old parental advice that sticks and stones can break your bones but words can never hurt you is simply bad advice. On the other hand, well-chosen words or speech for the benefit of good can motivate, inspiring others to greater feats and deeds. They can offer hope, create vision, impact others' beliefs and behavior, and alter the results of strategies, objectives, and, overall, people's lives.

Nationally syndicated columnist Peggy Noonan knows a thing or two about words and how they impact us. She recently wrote about the advice Clare Booth Luce once gave the newly inaugurated U.S. President John F. Kennedy. Luce was truly a remarkable woman. Her career spanned seven decades and nearly as many professional interests—journalism, politics, the theater, diplomacy, and intelligence.

According to Noonan, Luce had a conversation in the White House with her old friend John F. Kennedy in 1962. She told him, "A great man is one sentence." That is, his leadership can be so well summed up in a single sentence that you don't need to hear his name to know who's being talked about. Think of "He preserved the union and freed the slaves" and "He lifted us out of a great depression and helped win a world war." You don't need to be told that the answers are Lincoln and FDR.

Luce wondered what Kennedy's sentence would be. Her advice to him was to concentrate, to know the great themes and demands of his time, and focus on them. It was good advice. History has imperatives, and sometimes they are clear. Sometimes they are met, and sometimes not. When they're clear and met, you get quite a sentence (Noonan, *Wall Street Journal,* 26 June 2009).

Fast-forwarding to more contemporary times, the historic 2012 presidential debates might have had more significance than previous debates because of the words the candidates chose—their rhythm and nonverbal physical cues. A big part of successfully communicating depends on how well we negotiate the paradox of how the vast majority of human communication is conducted. We know from empirical research that more than 97 percent of human communication involves nonverbal cues (body language).

To give a successful presentation, speech, or presidential debate performance, we must compose a sophisticated but seamless message that unites our words in the proper rhythm and uses the corresponding nonverbal cues. If our words don't match our nonverbal cues, or vice versa, the audience will be confused and the message will be diminished—or, worse, ignored.

In the world of movies, theater, art, and entertainment, words have a dramatic impact. In a recent *Wall Street Journal* edition, a special report entitled "What's In a Name?" explored the original titles for a number of box office successes. For example, the Humphrey Bogart classic *Casablanca* had an original title of *Everybody Comes to Ricks.* The Julia Roberts/Richard Gere blockbuster *Pretty Woman* had an original title of *$3,000.* The successful *G.I. Jane* was slated to be released as *In Defense of Honor.* And the world might not have ever remembered Diane Keaton and Woody Allen in *Anhedonia,* but we do remember *Annie Hall* (*Wall Street Journal,* 19 October 2012, p. D1).

Words have the power to affect both the physical and emotional health of people to whom we speak, for better and for worse. Words used to influence are inspiring, uplifting, and challenging; they encourage, motivate, and persuade. They can be visionary; they can change people's lives for the better. Words used with power, coercion, force, and deception have a short-term impact, if they have any at all.

Verbal communication is a powerful human instrument, and we must learn to use it properly. We need to learn to think not only about *speaking* in new ways, but also about language, human nature, psychology, and sociology.

LET'S TAKE A MOMENT AND THINK ABOUT LANGUAGE

One of the peculiar characteristics of our culture involves how we communicate. Communication is perhaps the most important human function in which we engage, but we don't do it very well and aren't trained well to do so. We know that about 97 percent of human communication is through nonverbal cues or by use of mostly facial expressions and hand gestures. Because we don't trust our instincts driven by our amygdala (which some refer to as our animal brain) as much as we should, we have trouble absorbing the nonverbal human communications adequately.

Think about all our acculturation that teaches us to deny our amygdala-driven instincts: "We'll cross that bridge when we come to it," "Don't judge a book by its cover," "Don't jump to conclusions," "Look before you leap," "Act in haste, repent at your leisure," "We should have a committee meeting to talk it over first," and so on. In spite of how much communication nonverbal cues transfer, our schools provide very little training to improve human nonverbal perception.

For the 3 percent of human communication that is conveyed by language, we generally don't listen as effectively as we should. Furthermore, our educational system often fails students and society by giving them minimal instruction in communication skills (writing, speaking, and listening skills). Considering that we express almost every desire, need, emotion, feeling, want, expectation, demand, and frustration to other humans via communication, it is surprising and disappointing that lower forms of life do a better job of communicating.

WHAT IS THE SPECIAL SIGNIFICANCE OF LANGUAGE?

We learn language completely from audio cues—by listening. We do this because human brains are hard-wired, or genetically prewired, to learn language by listening as infants. Interestingly, we are not even consciously aware that we are cognitively learning. Before we had the ability to speak words, others could understand us. Our species survived and advanced by making other members understand with nonverbal cues. For more than a million years, children communicated to their mothers that they were hungry. Men communicated to women, and women to men, that they were interested in each other as partners. Hunters collaborated on big animal kills long before a word was spoken. Man even showed others how to start and keep a fire going long before there were words for such things. Anthropologists believe that the spoken word appeared on the scene between 350,000 B.C. and 160,000 B.C.—that's a long time spent using grunts, pointing, and relying on body language.

The special significance of language as a great idea lies in the fact that it is related to all other great ideas, insofar as ideas and thoughts are expressed to other persons mostly in language.

In his dialogues, Plato used Socrates as a character and continually called attention to the slippery nature of words and how sometimes words conceal thoughts as well as express them. In more modern times, philosophers such as Hobbes and Locke wrote about the abuse of words and how to use language. Today we view language a bit as an enemy—a barrier to communication and a tyranny of words. Debate even centers on whether communications and speech are the same thing.

A time will likely come when you have to give a presentation or speech. If you do not capture the attention of the audience with your communication skills, you will hear the crickets chirping because no one is listening to you. Then you will become another example of what not to say in a presentation. Maybe you are one of the lucky individuals who will not have to endure an interview or give a presentation. Nonetheless, you will have to communicate at some point. With the addition of texting, instant messaging, email, and social networking, we have few reasons to physically write a complete message and send it to a recipient anymore. However, if you choose to send a message, remember that it is a permanent reflection of you. This is how this book can help you.

History has seen many examples of memorable quotes that demonstrate that *how* someone says something is just as important as *what* he or she says. For example, when Lyndon B. Johnson was stumping for political office, he was asked the difference between himself and his opposing candidate. He famously replied, "He matriculated and I never matriculated." Some of the most famous speeches Abraham Lincoln made are memorable not just for their message, but also for the fact that Lincoln condensed an enormous amount of information into them. His second inaugural speech was a mere 700 words, and the *Gettysburg Address* was just under three minutes. Beyond his words, his cadence gave those speeches more power.

Power verbs express an action that is to be taken or that has been taken. Used correctly, a powerful verb has the power to impact your life, whether you are going into battle, running for president, or simply interviewing for a job.

Researchers have observed that, when students are given standardized tests and told that the tests are "intelligence exams," the average scores are 10 percent to 20 percent lower than when the same exam is given to similar students who are told that it is "just an exam."

We know that words create ideas, impressions, images, concepts, and facsimiles. Therefore, the words that we hear and read influence how we think and, consequently, how we behave. Thus, there is a correlation between the words we select and use and the results that occur.

The words we use, and the impact they have, can even be impacted by our background and other influences. Consider the words *buy* and *invest*. If you are selling life insurance, you want the customer to buy now, but in your mind, the purchase is a long-term investment. The premiums will be invested, the face value of the policy will grow, there will eventually be loan value, and the investment will appreciate beyond the purchase price. However, the customer thinks in terms of a purchase decision and how much it costs. The issue comes full circle if the customer does buy and wants the insurance company to make good investments with the premium.

Nan Russell, writing for Career Know-How, introduces this word choice: problem or challenge? Would you rather have your boss see your mistake as a problem or a challenge? Is it just semantics? Problems are fixed; challenges are met. Different words evoke a set of different emotions and different feelings. People usually have a much more positive feeling about "meeting a challenge" than "fixing a problem."

Power verbs can have medicinal benefits if used correctly, but consider this warning about words used inappropriately: They can actually cause individuals to become ill. In a published study on pain, researchers used functional magnetic resonance tomography (fMRI) to examine how 16 healthy people processed words associated with experiencing pain. The brain scans revealed which parts of the brain were activated in response to hearing the words. In the first experiment, researchers asked the participants to imagine situations that corresponded to words associated with pain (such as *excruciating, paralyzing,* and *grueling*), as well as situations that corresponded to negative but non-pain-associated words (such as *dirty* and *disgusting*) and both neutral and positive words. In the second experiment, the participants read the same words but were distracted by a brainteaser. In both cases, the results showed a clear response in the brain's pain-processing centers to the words associated with pain, but no such activity pattern arose in response to the other words. Researchers say that preserving painful experiences as memories in the brain might have been an evolutionary response to allow humans to avoid painful situations that might be dangerous (www.webmd.com/pain-management/news/20100402/words-really-do-hurt).

WEAVE IN BEAUTIFUL WORDS

What words make you feel warm and happy? Sure; it's different for all of us, but some words have universal appeal (at least, in English). The British

Council, which oversees education of the English language, conducts an annual study of the "Most Beautiful Words in the English Language." Forty-thousand people participated in the study. The top ten words were as follows:

1. Mother
2. Passion
3. Smile
4. Love
5. Eternity
6. Fantastic
7. Destiny
8. Freedom
9. Liberty
10. Tranquility

ADDITIONAL SUPPORT FOR YOU

For additional support, I have included eight words that Dr. Frank Luntz has complied from his research. These are words that have become powerful in the past ten years. The following list displays the words and briefly describes why they are powerful additions to your word arsenal.

1. *Consequences*: n. The phenomenon that follows, caused by a previous phenomenon.

2. *Impact:* n. A forceful consequence that causes listeners to assume that they will see and feel a measurable difference. Speaking about potential solutions or best effort is no longer good enough; people want results.

3. *Impact:* v. To have an effect upon, to cause listeners to assume that they will see and feel a measurable difference. Speaking about potential solutions or best effort is no longer good enough; people want results.

4. *Diplomacy:* n. A subtle, skillful, peaceful, nondramatic solution to problems. People are tired of drama, anxiety, and tension; they want leadership in diplomacy.

5. *Dialogue:* n. The discussion of diplomatic issues.

6. *Reliability:* n. The quality of being dependable in a way that was expected or better.

7. *Mission:* An authentic and genuine purpose.

8. *Commitment:* Dedication to what one promised.

In our American culture, a growing trend involves converting words that are nouns into verbs. *Verbed* has made its way into the mainstream and is used in everyday language. Some instances of this relate more to social media. The social networking site Facebook has also seen its name itself become a verb used to describe the action of communication. *Facebooking* someone now means sending a message or posting to someone's Wall. (Although my family believes that I am addicted to the social media site, they can be assured that, at all family functions, I will be the one taking all the photos and will later Facebook the photos. They will have clear copies, taken from a different perspective, for themselves for eternity.) Likewise, in the days before Facebook, to say you would "tag" someone meant something entirely different.

Another example of converting a noun to a verb is the search engine Google. Don't know the answer to something? Then *Google* it. The same can be said for texts. The action of sending a text has become shortened to the verb *texting.*

Especially for the millennial generation (born after 1970), people don't talk much on the phone anymore—they text each other. Although texting is fine for quick impersonal communications, it should never substitute for professional communication. This phenomenon of turning nouns into verbs means that the English language is constantly evolving and changing. Style manuals are outdated before they even hit the shelves, which is why this book is not a style manual: It does not attempt to identify these urbane, hip, or chic fad words. Instead, it includes a number of nouns that are now commonly accepted action verbs in today's business culture. Consider these examples:

silo	siloed
email	emailed
SPAM	spammed
message	messaged

The impact of action/power verbs and how they are woven into our collective conscience is evident in the names advertisers use for their products. For everyday items, we associate certain products with action verbs, as in these examples: Accord car model, Act mouthwash, Agree shampoo, Allure ski product, Ban deodorant, Budget Rent A Car, Converse tennis shoes, Dodge cars, Eclipse exercise machine, Endeavor spaceship, Edge shaving cream, Equal sugar substitute, Escalade Cadillac, Excel software, *Glamour* magazine, Gleem toothpaste, Google (company), Intuit software, Kindle e-reader, Marvel comics, Pilot pens, Pledge cleaner, Pioneer sound systems, Puff tissues, Quip (precursor to the fax machine), Raid bug killer, Shuffle iPod product, SPAM, Target store, and Vanish home cleaning product. These are just a few examples.

Over time, the inconsistency of English grammar has made it increasingly difficult for non-native speakers to learn English—even those who speak English as a first language often find it difficult to speak correctly. Some rules and styles are antiquated and not enforced. As a result, we have become lazy and are losing the war on poor grammar. English is a minefield of rules, and although I can assure you that this is not a style manual, it goes without saying that if you were to follow all the rules, you would spend a lifetime studying them. You'd also end up speaking a language that no normal person would understand. (And you'd be a complete bore.)

George Orwell wrote an essay in 1946 entitled "The Politics of the English Language," in which he criticized the ugly and inaccurate use of the English language, particularly the bland use of passive verbs:

> The passive voice is wherever possible used in preference to the active, and noun constructions are used instead of gerunds (*by examination of* instead of *by examining*). The range of verbs is further cut down by means of the *–ize* and *de–* formations, and the banal statements are given an appearance of profundity by means of the *not un–* formation. Simple conjunctions and prepositions are replaced by such phrases as *with respect to, having regard to, the fact that, by dint of, in view of, in the interests of, on the hypothesis that;* and the ends of sentences are saved by anticlimax by such resounding commonplaces as *greatly to be desired, cannot be left out of account, a development to be expected in the near future, deserving of serious consideration, brought to a satisfactory conclusion*, and so on and so forth. (Orwell, 1946)

As mentioned previously, the English language comes with many rules, and as with any rule, there are also exceptions, counterexceptions, special rules, do's and don'ts, and other confusing situations. More than 60 different rules and variations of rules exist for verbs alone. After you have learned the rules, you still have to follow exceptions. For example, consider the word *lightning* used as a verb. We say that it is "thundering and lightning all night"; it is the only exception to the rule that *–ing* can be added to the base verb to produce the *–ing* form. We do not say or write "It thundered and lightninging all night," nor do we say or write "It "thundered and lightning all night." As another exception to the rules, we say that we "relayed a message" but "relaid a carpet" (Crystal, 1995, p. 205).

For all my former English teachers and the dedicated writers of the grammar books on linguistic style and theory who will wonder why this book says nothing about active and passive voice, conjugation, and transitive or intransitive usage, that is your job. This guide is merely a road map to help individuals move toward success in everyday communications.

I am not excusing people from their responsibility and duty to learn the language correctly. However, there is a time and place for everything. Noam Chomsky, perhaps the most influential figure in the theoretical linguistics of the English language, recently conceived the goal of linguistics (all the rules, principles, and regulations) to be a description of the mental grammar of native speakers.

Chomsky perceives linguistics to be the system of all these rules, to characterize the mental structure that underlies our ability to speak and understand the language. Furthermore, Chomsky hypothesizes that humans have an innate language ability that enables children to quickly acquire a mental glimmer when they are exposed to a particular language. It's pretty amazing to think that a child learns an entire language by listening and observing some nonverbal cues. By the age of 5, a person has about 70 percent of lifetime vocabulary and linguistic rules learned by listening and observation.

Chomsky (and this is the last reference to a theorist or an intellectual, I promise) draws a distinction between competence in a language and performance in a language. Competence is the underlying knowledge of the theory and applications, whereas performance is the actual use of that knowledge. This book doesn't assume anything. It provides a performance tool for one part of the language: power verbs.

2

The Connection Between Success and Communications

Mountains of empirical evidence on two factors overwhelmingly account for the success of individuals in any field. Those two factors are verbal and networking skills.

Common sense and simple observation can be your laboratory. Just look at most of the successful people you know, have known, work with, or have worked for. Look at the people who ran or owned the organizations and firms for which you worked. Think about the people who owned and ran the vendor firms and organizations that serviced and supplied the firms and organizations for which you worked. What do most of these people have in common? The vast majority have bigger vocabularies and more extensive networks than you have. This primary reason likely explains why they are the business managers, leaders, and owners and the civic and social leaders.

It has long been known that successful executives do not have large useful vocabularies merely because of their position. Such a correlation is incorrect and does not properly explain cause and effect. In fact, the opposite is true. Successful executives (and successful people in other fields as well) are successful because their skills in vocabulary and networking give them tremendous help in advancing (Funk and Lewis, 1942, p. 3).

This guide is all about how power verbs can help make you a more effective communicator. Verbs are the catalysts of sentences. Verbs bring sentences to life. More to the point, the right action verbs bring your résumés, cover letters, speeches, presentations, networking contacts, sales plans, marketing plans, business and branding plans, and sales proposals to life. Frankly, the right power verbs can put a pop into all your interpersonal communications. The definitive source for the English language, the *Oxford English Dictionary,* states it this way:

> It is a simple truth that in most sentences you should
> express action through verbs, just as you do when you
> speak. Yet in so many sentences the verbs are smothered;
> all their vitality trapped beneath heavy noun phrases
> based on the verbs themselves. (AskOxford.com, 2008)

Dull and uninteresting verbs make communications of any type similarly dull and uninteresting. On the other hand, properly chosen action-packed verbs electrify your communications; they draw your listeners and readers to your topic and point of view like magnets.

Power verbs are useful in many ways, but this book focuses on helping you understand how to use power verbs more effectively where they really count:

- In speeches, presentations, and executive briefings
- In everyday communications
- In business documents, such as memos, reports, and plans
- In toasts and impromptu comments
- In networking communications

No other convenient source has as complete a list of action verbs or as effective an explanation of usage. The power verbs in this book describe a proactive approach to some issue, problem, or need. (For example, she *accelerated* the strategic plan with her visionary thinking.)

However, some action verbs included here are not explicitly positive in their form (such as the verbs *limited* and *composed*), but they are included because they can show a proactive approach to cutting, stopping, halting, reversing, or limiting some negative issue or problem, or creating an alternative positive environment. (For example, she *limited* the costs of new product development.) Similarly, some contemporary words, idioms, and phrases, such as *emailed* and *walk the walk*, reflect the contemporary lexicon, regardless of whether they all pass the smell test of proper grammar.

Many action verbs in this compilation might appear to not fit the premise stated above: Power verbs such as *cannibalize, bankrupt, disgrace, rape,* and *prevaricate* certainly do not appear to be positive. However, this compilation is not just a collection of happy-sounding words—life doesn't work that way. We live and work and communicate in a rough-and-tumble world. Our communications need to be fresh and crisp, yet they do not need to reflect street lingo or sound overwhelmingly "hip." These power verbs are meant to help you inject spark and life into your communications and give your communications special impact.

Throughout the book, the power verbs are shown in the present tense with two inflected forms: verbs ending in *–end* and *–in*. However, as the examples throughout show, the tense in which you would use them depends on the circumstance and the situation.

The following chapters feature an alphabetical list of more than 500 power verbs, divided into broad categories of human knowledge to make finding the right word easier.

PRONUNCIATION NOTES

The English language, and especially the American form, has derived from many other languages, including Greek; Latin; Hebrew; several versions of Spanish, French, German; and some native American tongues. Add in the regional variations, and it is no wonder that English has few hard-and-fast rules of pronunciation.

But although America is a diverse culture, English is still the language of business. Therefore, the action verbs in this guide and the pronunciation notes generally follow the Merriam–Webster pronunciation guidelines. However the author has added features not used by Merriam–Webster.

VERB FORMS

Progressive Forms

Present progressive tense: Verbs showing ONGOING ACTION

The present progressive tense describes an ongoing action that is happening at the same moment for which the action is being written. To form this tense, one uses *am/is/are* with the verb form ending in *–ing*.

Examples:

> I <u>am meeting</u> with the others tomorrow.
>
> The project management team <u>is examining</u> the stakeholder's proposal.
>
> The team members <u>are researching</u> ideation options.
>
> She <u>is</u> happy.

Use the present tense to describe something that is true regardless of time.

Past progressive tense: Verbs showing SIMULTANEOUS ACTION

The past progressive tense that describes an action that was happening when another action occurred. To form this tense, use *was/were* with the verb form ending in *–ing*.

Examples:

> The new project team <u>was presenting</u> its recent findings when the power went out.

Four team members <u>were meeting</u> with the sponsor when the news broke about the award.

Future progressive tense: Verbs showing FUTURE ACTION

The future progressive tense describes an action that is ongoing or continuous and one that will take place in the future. To form this, use *will be* or *shall be* with the verb form ending in *–ing*.

Examples:

Only one team member <u>will be presenting</u> during the annual meeting in June.

The clock <u>is</u> ticking, the band <u>is</u> playing.

When the progressive form is not used for continuing events, a dramatic style effect can be produced:

The clock <u>ticks</u>.

The band <u>plays</u>.

Present perfect progressive: Verbs showing PAST ACTION, CONTINUOUS ACTION, and POSSIBLY ONGOING ACTION

The present perfect progressive tense describes an action that began in the past, continues in the present, and might continue into the future. To form this tense, use *has/have been* and the present participle of the verb (the verb form ending in *–ing*).

Example:

The project sponsor <u>has been considering</u> an increase in the budget.

Past perfect progressive: Verbs showing PAST ACTION and an ONGOING ACTION COMPLETED BEFORE SOME OTHER PAST ACTION

The past perfect progressive tense describes a past, ongoing action that was completed before some other past action. This tense is formed by using *had been* and the present perfect of the verb (the verb form ending in *–ing*).

Example:

Before the budget increase, the project team <u>had been participating</u> in many sponsor meetings.

Future perfect progressive: Verbs showing ONGOING ACTION OCCURRING BEFORE SOME SPECIFIED TIME

The future perfect progressive tense describes a future, ongoing action that will occur before some specified future time. This tense is formed by using *will have been* and the present participle of the verb (the verb form ending in *–ing*).

Example:

> By the next fiscal year, the new product develop project team <u>will have been researching</u> and <u>proposing</u> more than 60 new product categories.

The following chapters display power verbs with the action verb, its pronunciation, up to two forms of the inflected verb (perfect and progressive), and several synonyms.

All verbs are listed in active form. Although there are effective and appropriate times and places for passive verbs (as in "Professor, I was robbed of an A grade!"), active voice is preferred because it is clear and concise and gets quickly to the point (as in "The professor gave Ron a B for the course").

If you want to learn more about when and how to use active and passive verbs, get yourself a good grammar or style book.

Recognize an intransitive verb **when you see one.**

An intransitive verb has two characteristics. First, it is an <u>action verb</u>, expressing a doable activity such as **arrive, go, lie, sneeze, sit,** and **die.** Second, unlike a <u>transitive verb</u>, it does not have a <u>direct object</u> to receive the action.

Consider these examples of intransitive verbs:

> Huffing and puffing, we **arrived** at the church with only seconds to spare.
>
> **arrived** = intransitive verb
>
> Jorge **went** to the campus cafe for a bowl of hot chicken noodle soup.
>
> **went** = intransitive verb
>
> To escape the midday heat, the dogs **lie** in the shade under our trees.
>
> **lie** = intransitive verb
>
> Around fresh ground pepper, Sheryl **sneezes** with violence.
>
> **sneezes** = intransitive verb
>
> In the early morning, Mom **sits** on the front porch to admire her beautiful flowers.
>
> **sits** = intransitive verb
>
> Flipped on its back, the roach that Dee dosed with pest repellent **dies** under the stove.
>
> **dies** = intransitive verb

3

How to Use This Book

If you have a presentation or speech to give, you should know the basic rules for every presentation. Other sources on presentations might use different guidelines, but these rules are summarized from 35 years of personal experience and research.

1. Know your audience. You must know who will be listening to you. Why have these people given up their time to come hear you? What do they expect to get out of hearing your presentation? What do they expect to take away from your presentation?

2. Prepare, prepare, prepare. Research your topic so that you feel comfortable *talking* about it. Delve into the background, history, trends, and current issues. Have a working knowledge of the critical facts and details to support the points you intend to make.

3. Rehearse, rehearse, rehearse. You do not want to recite or read your presentation; you want to appear to have given it several times before. If you have delivered it in dress rehearsal format at least six times, you will look well rehearsed.

4. In the presentation, use notes; do not read your presentation.

5. If you use slides, do not look back at the slides; maintain eye contact with the audience.

6. Select an appropriate tone, style, pitch, rate, and time.

7. From the following lists, carefully select powerful verbs that add punch to your sentences.

Power verbs for speakers and presenters are arranged alphabetically under major and minor categories of human knowledge.[1]

We call familiarity with someone or something "human knowledge," and this can include facts, information, descriptions, analysis of data, or skills acquired through experience or education. Furthermore, it can refer to the

---

[1] Based on *The Outline of Knowledge*, edited by Mortimer J. Adler.

theoretical (the explicit) or practical (implicit) understanding of a subject. The author has included hundreds of the most useful power verbs as part of the practical implicit piece of human knowledge, to help speakers and presenters pump up their speeches, toasts, briefings, talks, impromptu remarks, and other forms of human communications.

You must put together the rest of your sentences using good grammar, style, syntax, and tense, but the power and sway of your sentences and phrases come from your power verbs.

When searching for attention-grabbing, highly impactful power verbs, think about your topic or subject of interest and then consult this book by first searching for the appropriate broad category of human knowledge (Art, Morals and Ethics, Technology, and so on). Then refine your search by looking in the subcategories for just the right power verbs. The power verbs that will pump up your communications are listed alphabetically under the categories and subcategories.

To find the right power verbs, cross-check the selected power verbs and other main categories and subcategories of human knowledge in the index. Uncommonly used power verbs include an international pronunciation.

Each power verb has synonyms and abbreviated definitions to help you position just the right power verbs for the impact and effect you desire. See the following example.

DESPOIL

(1)   damage; deface; defile; overexploit; pillage; plunder; ravage; rob; ruin; steal; spoil; wreck; vandalize

> *(1)*   *"Critics, including the Sonoma County Board of Supervisors, say the tribe's plans to build 'Rancho San Pablo' would **despoil** the natural beauty of the area—one of the Bay Area's last large undeveloped bayside vistas. —Jim Doyle, Pomo Indians Plan Housing Tract on San Pablo Bay Land, San Francisco Chronicle, p. A15, 15 January 1996.*

> *(2)*   *"Aristotle said: 'Men come together in cities in order to live, but they remain together in order to live the good life.' It is harder and harder to live the good life in American cities today. The catalog of ills is long: there is the decay of the centers and the **despoiling** of the suburbs. — President Lyndon Baines Johnson, The Great Society Speech, Ann Arbor, Michigan. 22 May 1964.*

> Collocates to: environment, lands, natural beauty, open space, parklands, wetlands, wilderness

In most cases, the power verbs have examples of the specific word in actual use. These examples include the power verb used in sentences, famous speeches, quotations, and newspaper and magazine articles. Some power verbs have a list of words that collocate or tend to be grouped with that power verb.

In addition to these aids, where possible and appropriate, examples of using the power verb in more vivid language phrasing and form are included. These include

- **Alliteration:** The repetition of the consonant sound of close or adjoining words. An example of alliteration is "Step forward, Tin Man. You dare to come to me for a heart, do you? You <u>c</u>linking, <u>c</u>lanking, <u>c</u>lattering <u>c</u>ollection of <u>c</u>aliginous junk. … And you, Scarecrow, have the effrontery to ask for a <u>b</u>rain! You <u>b</u>illowing <u>b</u>ale of <u>b</u>ovine fodder!" —Delivered by Frank "Wizard of Oz" Morgan (from the movie *The Wizard of Oz*).

- **Antithesis:** The juxtaposition of contrasting ideas frequently in parallel structure. Examples might include, "Ask not what your country can do for you; ask what you can do for your country." —John Kennedy. Another example is, "All men dream, but not equally. Those who dream by night in the dusty recesses of their minds, wake in the day to find that it was vanity: but the dreamers of the day are dangerous men, for they may act on their dreams with open eyes, to make them possible." —T. E. Lawrence.

- **Metaphor:** An implicit comparison between things that are essentially different yet have something in common. It is different from the simile, in that the metaphor does not contain words such as *like* or *as*. Examples of metaphors might include "The same sun warms rich and poor," "Great managers manage by chess, good managers manage by checkers," "Life is journey; travel it well," and "Life is a zoo in a jungle."

- **Parallelism:** A pair or series of related words, phrases, or sentences. An example of parallelism might be "We **defeated** communism. We **defeated** fascism. We **defeated** them on the field of battle, and we **defeated** them on the field of ideas." —Colin Powell.

- **Repetition:** The same word or set of words repeated at the beginning or end of successive sentences, phrases, or clauses. Repetition usually results in parallelism and builds a strong cadence in the speaker's delivery. An example of repetition is "We will not tire, we will not falter, and we will not fail." —George W. Bush. Another example is "The ever important murmur, dramatize it, dramatize it!" —Henry James, American expatriate writer (1843–1916).

- **Simile:** An explicit comparison between things that are essentially different yet have something in common. Similes always includes a word such as *like* or *as*. Examples include "busy as a bee," "hungry as a tiger," and "light as a feather." Overuse of similes creates clichés and diminishes the vivid impression you are trying to create.

Following are some examples from the book:

ACHIEVE

(1)   accomplish; attain; complete; conclude; do; finish; get; reach; perform; pull off; realize

(2)   succeed in doing something

   (1), (2) *"The results you **achieve** will be in direct proportion to the effort you apply." —Denis Waitley*

Alliteration: If you help others **a**ccomplish their goals and **a**ttain their objectives, you will **achieve** your dreams.

Parallelism: "Some people are born mediocre, some people **achieve** mediocrity, and some people have mediocrity thrust upon them." —Joseph Heller

Repetition: If you want to **achieve,** you have to rise early; if you want **achieve,** you have to work hard every day; if you want to **achieve,** you have to accomplish something every day before you go to sleep.

COEXIST

(1)   to peacefully exist together or side by side

   (1)   *During the Cold War, the major powers determined **coexistence** was preferable to the alternative, which could have been a nuclear holocaust.*

Antithesis: "In economics, hope and faith **coexist** with great scientific pretension and also a deep desire for respectability." —John Kenneth Galbraith

Antithesis: "The present and the past **coexist,** but the past shouldn't be in flashback." —Alain Resnais

Parallelism: "The only alternative to **coexistence** is codestruction." —Jawaharlal Nehru, Indian Prime Minister (1889–1964)

Repetition: "I think sometimes when children grow up, their parents grow up. Mine grew up with me. We **coexist**. I don't try to change them anymore, and I don't think they try to change me. We agree to disagree." —Katy Perry, singer

ATTACK

(1) approach; assail; attempt to launch an assault; blast; fire; flank; onrush; onset; set upon; snipe

(2) to set to work on; to take the initiative and go on the offensive

Alliteration: "Men rise from one **a**mbition to another: first, they seek to secure themselves **a**gainst **attack**, **a**nd then they **attack** others." —Niccolo Machiavelli, Italian writer and statesman, Florentine patriot, and author of *The Prince* (1469–1527)

Antithesis: "Invincibility lies in the defense; the possibility of victory in the **attack**." —Sun Tzu, Chinese general and author (b. 500 B.C.)

Metaphor: "Yesterday, December 7th, 1941—a date which will live in infamy—the United States of America was suddenly and deliberately **attacked** by naval and air forces of the Empire of Japan." —President Franklin Roosevelt, *Pearl Harbor Address* to the nation, Washington, D.C., 8 December 1941

Repetition: "Nobody ever defended anything successfully, there is only **attack** and **attack** and **attack** some more." —Gen. George S. Patton, American general in World War I and World War II (1885–1945)

Repetition: "Yesterday, the Japanese government also launched an attack against Malaya. Last night, Japanese forces **attacked** Hong Kong. Last night, Japanese forces **attacked** Guam. Last night, Japanese forces **attacked** the Philippine Islands. Last night, the Japanese **attacked** Wake Island. And this morning, the Japanese **attacked** Midway Island." —President Franklin Roosevelt, *Pearl Harbor Address* to the nation, Washington, D.C., 8 December 1941

Simile: **Attack** *as* viciously as a lioness attacking a gazelle in search of a meal for her cubs.

Now go search for the power verbs that will pump up your verbal communications!

4

Art/Particular Visual Art Forms: Acting, Dance, Music, Painting and Printmaking, Photography, Publishing, and Writing

ACTING, PERFORMING, AND VISUAL ART

ABREACT (â-brē-ăkt)

(1)   ally; ease; release repressed emotions by acting out in words; behavior or imagining the relief; situation; still

   (1)   Jose was asked by his therapist to <u>abreact</u> his dreams he had been having about his childhood.

ACCENTUATE

(1)   accent; emphasize; heighten; intensify; mark with an accent

   (1) Kim has to manipulate shading and depth of field so that she can <u>accentuate</u> certain artistic elements in her photos.

   (1) <u>Accentuate</u> the sweet smell of success. ["<u>s</u>weet <u>s</u>mell of <u>s</u>uccess" is an example of alliteration]

(2)   play up; make more noticeable; stress something; make prominent

   (2) The theater's pricing policies merely <u>accentuated</u> the power of the market principle.

   (1), (2) "A science is said to be useful if its <u>d</u>evelopment tends to <u>accentu-</u><u>ate</u> the existing inequities in the <u>d</u>istribution of wealth, or more <u>d</u>irectly

promotes the destruction of human life." ("development tends to accentu-
ate the existing inequities in the distribution of wealth, or more directly
promotes the destruction of human life" is an example of alliteration)
—Godfrey Harold Hardy, A Mathematician's Apology

Collocates to: differences, further, lines, negative, positive, shape, skills, tends

ACCOMPANY

(1)   add to; attend; convoy; escort; go along; go with; journey with

(2)   be an adjunct with; complement; go together with; perform with; send
      with; supplement; tied to

      (1), (2) It is an honor to accompany a famous artist.

      *(1), (2) "They are never alone that are accompanied with noble
      thoughts." —Philip Sidney,* An Apology of Poetry, or a Defense of Poesy,
      Book I *(1581)*

Parallelism: When you accompany a diva, you accompany greatness, you
accompany history.

ACHIEVE

(1)   accomplish; attain; complete; conclude; do; finish; get; reach; perform;
      pull off; realize

(2)   succeed in doing something

      *(1), (2) "The results you achieve will be in direct proportion to the effort
      you apply." —Denis Waitley, American speaker and consultant specializ-
      ing in motivation, early 1930s*

Alliteration: "If you help others accomplish their goals and attain their objectives, you will achieve your dreams."

Vivid imagery: "No man or woman is an island. To exist just for yourself is
meaningless. You can achieve the most satisfaction when you feel related to
some greater purpose in life, something greater than yourself." —Denis
Waitley

Parallelism: "Some people are born mediocre, some people achieve mediocrity, and some people have mediocrity thrust upon them." —Joseph Heller,
American author

Repetition: "If you want to achieve, you have to rise early; if you want to
achieve, you have to work hard every day; if you want to achieve, you have to
accomplish something every day before you go to sleep." —Unknown

ACT

(1) act out; appear in; feign; impersonate; mock; perform; play in; pretend; simulate

(1) Professor Kim's goal was to have her students look like, sound like, think like, and act like their character.

(1) "Everybody who tells you how to act has whisky on their breath." —John Hoyer Updike, author, Rabbit, Run

(1) "Save something for the third act." —Anonymous show business adage applied by President Reagan to his final months in the White House; quoted in Time, *16 March 1987*

(1) "The four most dramatic words in the English language: 'Act One, Scene One.'" —Moss Hart, Act One

Vivid imagery: "All men dream, but not equally. Those who dream by night in the dusty recesses of their minds, wake in the day to find that it was vanity: but the dreamers of the day are dangerous men, for they may act on their dreams with open eyes, to make them possible." —T. E. Lawrence, author, poet, spy

Metaphor: "The possibilities are numerous once we decide to act and not react." —George Bernard Shaw, Irish literary critic, playwright, essayist, and winner of 1925 Nobel Prize for Literature (1856–1950)

AD-LIB

(1) extemporize; improvise words not in prepared speech; make up on the spot; unprompted remarks

(1) Many ad-lib comments turn out to have been scripted all along.

AMUSE

(1) absorb; beguile; engross; entertain; distract; divert; interest; keep amused or busy; occupy; recreate

(2) charm; divert; please; make laugh or smile

(1), (2) "Why does one never hear of government funding for the preservation and encouragement of comic strips, girlie magazines and TV soap operas? Because these genres still hold the audience they were created to amuse and instruct." —John Hoyer Updike, New York Review of Books, *18 July 1984*

Collocates to: friends, oneself, others, people, seem, trying, ways

Parallelism: "You make 'em, I amuse them." —Dr. Seuss, American writer and cartoonist

Repetition: "To get into the best society nowadays, one has either to feed people, amuse people, or shock people." —Oscar Wilde, Irish poet, novelist, dramatist, and critic (1854–1900)

Vivid imagery: "Amuse the reader at the same time that you instruct him." Horace, Roman poet (65 B.C.–8 B.C.)

ANIMATE

(1)   give life to; give sprit and support to; quicken

(2)   make or design in such a way as to create apparently spontaneous lifelike movement

> *(1), (2) "The object of literature is to instruct, to animate, or to amuse."*
> *—George Henry Lewis, author*

AUDITION

(1)   test; trial performance; trial; tryout

> *(1) "I don't think actors should ever expect to get a role, because the disappointment is too great. You've got to think of things as an opportunity. An audition's an opportunity to have an audience." —Al Pacino, actor*

BACKLIGHT

(1)   light, or illuminate, from the rear or from

> *(1) This is backlight technology.*

> *(1) Even in dim light, you need not use backlight.*

BARNSTORM

(1)   conduct a campaign in rural areas by making brief stops in many small towns; moving from location to location with entertainment, sports, or other attraction without a lot of preparation

> *(1) What a barnstorming finish!*

> *(1) The presidential candidates spend the year before the election barnstorming the swing states.*

BEGUILE

(1)   attract; betray; bluff; charm into doing; deceive; delude; divert; enthrall; entice; fascinate; lure; manipulate; mesmerize; mislead; put under a spell; string along; woo

(1) "The reason of idleness and of crimes is the deferring of our hopes. Whilst we are waiting, we beguile the time with jokes, with sleep, with eating and with crimes." —Ralph Waldo Emerson, U.S. essayist, poet, and philosopher (1803–1882); "Nominalist and Realist," Essays, Second Series (1844)

Alliteration: You can betray, bluff, and beguile your way to the top, but be prepared for a quick trip back to the bottom.

Vivid imagery: "I am not merry, but I do beguile." —William Shakespeare, English dramatist, playwright, and poet (1564–1616)

BLOVIATE

(1)   hold forth in a pompous, self-centered way; orate verbosely; speak pompously and at length

(1) To bloviate is not recommended when you are among experts on the current topic.

(1) "Warren Harding invented the word 'normalcy,' and the lesser known 'bloviate,' meaning one imagines, to spout, to spew aimless verbiage." —John Ashbery, U.S. poet and critic (1927–)

CAKE CUT (slang)

(1)   carny slang for short-changing customers; crank; strom

(1) Will Rogers warned us that politicians frequently find their hands in our pockets, a condition similar to being cake cut at a carnival by a flim-flam artist.

CANTILLATE

(1)   chant or recite in musical monotone; hum in a low tone

(1) The cantor began to cantillate according to the traditional Jewish melody.

CONCINNATE

(1) arrange or blend skillfully, as parts or elements; put together in a harmonious, precisely appropriate, or elegant manner; show skill and harmony, especially in a literary work; show an elegant arrangement

(1) The commission may, however, publish the terms of conciliation because it was <u>concinnated</u> and completely agreeable to both parties.

DEBUT

(1) appear for the first time; entrance; introduction; make debut; presentation; unveiling

(1) She decided to <u>debut</u> with several other violinists.

(1) The book <u>debuted</u> at number one on the New York Times Best Seller List.

DRAMATIZE

(1) adapt for the stage; aggrandize; blow up; embellish; exaggerate; lay it on thick; lard; overstate; perform; play up; produce; sensationalize; stage

(1) <u>Dramatize</u> the great human emotions in relation to the dynamics of the city.

Metaphor: "In Europe life is histrionic and dramatized, and … in America, except when it is trying to be European, it is direct and sincere." —William Dean Howell, American realist author and literary critic; nicknamed "The Dean of American Letters" (1837–1920)

Repetition: "The ever important murmur, "<u>dramatize</u> it, <u>dramatize</u> it!" —Henry James, American expatriate writer (1843–1916)

Vivid imagery: "The most dramatic conflicts are perhaps those that take place not between men, but between a man and himself—where the arena of conflict is a solitary mind." —Clark Moustakas, American psychologist and one of the leading experts on humanistic and clinical psychology (1923–2012)

<u>Collocates to: attempts, character, effective, event, order, plight, scene, situation</u>

DUKKER (slang)

(1) carny slang for fortune telling

(1) The carnival worker was <u>dukkering</u> but was not a Delphic Oracle, nor was it some sort of Magical Mystery Tour.

EXTEMPORIZE

(1) ad-lib; divagate; perform or act in an impromptu manner; improvise; manage in a makeshift way; perform without permission or preparations; speak off the cuff; speak or perform at a moment's notice

(1) "It is safer to accept any chance that offers itself, and <u>extemporize</u> a procedure to fit it, than to get a good plan matured and wait for a chance of using it." —Thomas Hardy, British novelist and poet (1840–1928)

(1) "Sometimes, for days and even weeks, there would be the illusion of progress. In the drawer below the one where he kept his notebooks, he had sketches and outlines galore. He'd even fully orchestrated one or two passages, although he'd known even at the time he was doing them that he was simply playing at composition, producing something he could show visitors and <u>extemporize</u> around on the piano." —Ian R. MacLeod, "The Noonday Pool," Fantasy & Science Fiction 88, issue 5, May 1995, p. 68

(1) After the flood, we had to <u>extemporize</u> for weeks.

Vivid imagery: "It is safer to accept any chance that offers itself, and <u>extemporize</u> a procedure to fit it, than to get a good plan matured and wait for a chance of using it." —Thomas Hardy, British novelist and poet (1840–1928)

FOURWALL

(1) pay for the right to entertain at a theater or on a stage.

(1) "In Vegas parlance, Wallace is a '<u>four-waller</u>,' the term used when an entertainer pays for his or her stage time." —Sam Howe Verhovek, Los Angeles Times, 20 March 2006

GO DARK

(1) shut down or cancel performances

(1) The theater may have to <u>go dark</u> if ticket sales do not pick up.

LIMN

(1)   depict or describe in paintings or words

(1) They are rated by their ability to <u>limn</u> the customer's likeness on paper.

MAIL IT IN

(1)   dial it in; go through the motions; perform in a cursory or substandard manner

(1) Based on his effort in rehearsals for the performance, it appeared as though he had decided to <u>mail it in</u>.

OIL SPOT

(1)   accidentally leave behind a member of a touring company or road show

(1) For roadies, truck stops provide a place to frolic, shop, and occasionally get <u>oil spotted</u>.

(1) Ronda was a big fan, but to the band, she was just another <u>oil spot</u> they could leave at a diner without another thought.

SCULPT

(1)   carve; create; craft; design; form; shape; manipulate

(1) He will sculpt because he is an artist.

Repetition: "In film, we <u>sculpt</u> time, we <u>sculpt</u> behavior, and we <u>sculpt</u> light."
—David Fencher, American film and music video director (1962–)

Metaphor: "I paint and <u>sculpt</u> to get a grip on reality … to protect myself."
—Alberto Giacometti, Swiss sculptor, painter, draughtsman, and printmaker (1902–1966)

SUBLIMATE

(1)   distill; divert the energy of a primitive impulse into a culturally higher activity; make pure; purify; refine; sublime

(1) <u>Sublimate</u> this urge by the solving of artificial puzzles devised for our entertainment.

Metaphor: "The human spirit <u>sublimates</u> the impulses it thwarts; a healthy sex life mitigates the lust for other sports." —Piet Hein, Danish inventor (1905–1996)

Collocates to: directly, goals, individual, negative, love, self, urges

DANCE

AMAGAR

(1) to fake a dance move

(1) There is no way to amagar a Martha Graham dance step.

CHOREOGRAPH

(1) arrange; compose; direct

Simile: "Dancers are instruments, *like a* piano the choreographer plays."
—George Balanchine, one of the 20th century's most famous choreographers, a developer of ballet in the United States, and the cofounder and balletmaster of New York City Ballet (1904–1983)

FIRE DANCE

(1) an exotic form of dancing

FREE STYLE

(1) dance in an ad-lib fashion; do dance movements with no fixed structure and dance to a variety of music styles

LINDY BOMB

(1) swing-dance as a group in a place where it is not normally done

PHRASE

(1) fit specific dance figures to the rhythm and/or melody of the music

(1) Phrasing may be adjusted in certain dances by the use of lead-in steps to bring the dancers in on a different beat.

SHIMMY

(1) shaking of the shoulders and the whole body

MUSIC

ACCENT

(1) emphasize; make a particular part more important

AURALIZE

(1)   hear mentally; imagine the sound of

(1) I often auralize new songs in my mind.

BEAT TIME

(1)   mark musical time by beating a drum, clapping, tapping the foot, or similar means

(1) Street musicians frequently beat time on boxes, buckets, and other percussion devices.

CANTILLATE

(1)   chant or recite in musical monotone; declaim in singsong; intonate

DESCANT

(1)   play a melody or part different than the main

ENCORE

(1)   do again; perform the relevant passage once more

(1) This was the first time I've heard of the band doing a second encore.

HARMONIZE

(1)   accommodate; accord; agree; attune; bring into consonance or accord; conform; coordinate; integrate; proportion; reconcile; tune

(1) "Hatred paralyzes life; love releases it. Hatred confuses life; love harmonizes it. Hatred darkens life; love illuminates it." (example of repetition) —Martin Luther King, Jr., American Baptist minister and civil rights leader (1929–1968)

(1) "The fundamental facts of mechanics do not harmonize with this view.

Antithesis: "There is not in all the pulpit's ingenuity enough to harmonize these ignorant and stupid contradictions." —Robert Green Ingersoll, American statesman and orator (1833–1899)

Collocates to: colors, efforts, interests, laws, music, polices, regulations, taxes, tones, together

MASH UP

(1)   combine songs or digital content into a new file

(2)   brew or infuse

(3)   combine two or more Web sites into a single site

SOLO

(1)   do something alone; executed by a single instrument or voice

Antithesis: "Sometimes it's better to be <u>solo</u> than work with people who are gonna hold you back from achievement." —Robert Escalate, founder and owner of Escalate retail

Simile: "Life is *like* playing a violin <u>solo</u> in public and learning the instrument as one goes on." —Samuel Butler, English novelist, essayist, and critic (1835–1902)

PAINTING/PRINTMAKING

GRANGERIZE

(1)   illustrate a published book with drawings, illustrations, pictures, engravings, prints, and pictures obtained elsewhere, often from other books

(2)   mutilate a book by cutting out its illustrations

KING

(1)   among graffiti artists, to (pervasively) paint one's name or symbol (throughout an area); to own an area through tagging or bombing

PHOTOGRAPHY

EAT UP THE CAMERA

(1)   in movies, to be appealing or engaging on screen

   (1) No one could better <u>eat up the camera</u> than Marilyn Monroe.

PAP

(1)   take a photograph of someone or something

ABBREVIATE

(1)   abridge; clip; compress; condense; curtail; cut back; digest; diminish; pare; reduce; shorten; truncate

(2)   make specific initials or an acronym out of a word or phrase

(1), (2) Don't <u>abbreviate</u> a word one time and spell it out another time in the same paragraph.

AUTHOR

(1)   create; pen; scribe; source; write

(1) Do you have a favorite <u>author</u> whom you admire or who has influenced your work?

Antithesis: "He who purposes to be an <u>author</u> should first be a student." —John Dryden (1631–1700)

BOUSTROPHEDON (bōō'strō fē'dən)

(1)   write text so that each line is in an alternate direction

BOWDLERIZE

(1)   censor; edit; expurgate; remove obscenity or other inappropriate content

(1) In the 1960s, the school board of my town wanted to <u>bowdlerize</u> the classic novel Tom Jones.

GHOST-WRITE

(1)   write something in another's name

(1) She agreed to <u>ghost-write</u> the governor's autobiography.

JOURNAL

(1)   create a daily record of thoughts, impressions, and autobiographical information, often as a source of ideas for writing

Vivid imagery: <u>Journal</u> writing is a voyage to the interior.

OFFSET (also see Nature)

(1) cause printed material to transfer or smear onto another surface

(2) compensate for or counterbalance something

(3) make up for

PASTICHE

(1) combine various works or styles into a mixture or hodgepodge

PIPE

(1) embellish, fabricate, or invent information for a newspaper article

> (1) "Jim Roberts's research also established the likelihood of inaccuracies, plagiarism, piped quotes, and faked datelines in many other Blair stories." —Howard Raines, "My Times," The Atlantic, June 2004

PROMULGATE

(1) broadcast; circulate; publish or make known; spread; transmit

Collocates to: beliefs, falsehoods, the faith, information, lies, rules, regulations, propaganda, truth

REPURPOSE

(1) convert content designed for print media and into a Web-based format; reformat; transfer

RETCON

(1) retroactively revise (a plot, storyline, character, event, history, and so on), usually by reinterpreting past events or theorizing how the present would be different if past events either had not happened or had happened differently

5

The Earth and Nature: Earth's Properties, History, Structure, and Composition

ADAPT

(1)   make fit for; change to suit a new purpose

(2)   change or conform oneself to new or different conditions

   (1), (2) Intelligence is the ability to <u>adapt</u> to change. —Stephen Hawking, British theoretical physicist, cosmologist, and author (1942–)

Antithesis: "<u>Adapt</u> or perish, now as ever, is nature's inexorable imperative." —H. G. Wells, American writer

Antithesis: "Unfortunately in the past, if you had a special need, you had to <u>adapt</u> to the machine." —David Bear

Simile: "The wise <u>adapt</u> themselves to circumstances, *as* water molds itself to the pitcher." —Chinese proverb

Vivid imagery: "<u>Adapt</u> yourself to the things among which your lot has been cast and love sincerely the fellow creatures with whom destiny has ordained that you shall live." —Marcus Aurelius, Roman emperor (AD 121–180)

CALCIFY

(1)   change into a hard, stony substance

(2)   turn into lime

(3)   become inflexible and unchanging

   (3) "Rumors are the backbone of what Michael Taussig (1992) calls 'the nervous system.' (n2) In violent and dangerous situations the throng of rumors told over and over and over <u>calcify</u> into accepted representations of social reality and political life." Glen A. Perice, "Rumors and Politics in Haiti," Anthropological Quarterly *70, issue 1, January 1997, p. 1–10*

CARBON CAPTURE

(1) capture CO_2 from a process before it is emitted into the atmosphere, and usually store it in the ground

(1) "CEO Michael G. Morris said AEP and its partners have advanced carbon capture technology more than any other power generator, but at this time it doesn't make economic sense to continue." —Ken Wells and Ben Elgin, "What's Killing Carbon Capture," Bloomberg BusinessWeek Magazine, *21 July 2011*

CARBON DATE

(1) date the age of a fossil or an artifact by measuring the content of radioactive carbon

(1) Archeologists can use a scientific test to identify the carbon date of many artifacts, such as bone, cloth, wood, and plant fibers, that were created in the relatively recent past by human activities.

CHERRY STEM

(1) extend a spur of unprotected nonwilderness land, especially a dead-end road or trail, through a protected wilderness area

(1) "Mr. Dodson said the plan 'cherry stemmed' many wilderness areas, drawing boundaries along existing roads so that it is possible to penetrate close to the center." —Robert Reinhold, New York Times, *10 June 1988*

CLONE

(1) make an identical copy of an original organism or thing

(1) Many organisms naturally reproduce by making clones of themselves as a form of asexual reproduction.

Collocates to: animals, embryos, genetics, humans, ideas, mammals, pets, stem cells, twins

DELUGE

(1) drench; flood; flow over completely; great rainfall; inundate; saturate; soak; swamp

Collocates to: digital communications, complaints, flood, job applications, lawsuits, publicity, rain, résumés

DESICCATE

(1)   burn; dehydrate; dry out; scorch; wither

DISPERSE

(1)   go in different directions; distribute loosely; move away from one another; separate

(1) Organisms may disperse as spores, seeds, eggs, larvae, or adults.

(2)   be widely known

Collocates to: animals, birds, capital, clouds, crowds, demonstrators, marchers, mobs, oil slicks, people, soldiers

EMIT *(also see Education, Communication, and Law)*

(1)   expel gas

(2)   give off, send forth, or discharge

(3)   express audibly

Collocates to: carbon dioxide, emissions, gases, gamma, glow, infrared, odor, particles, pollutants, radiation, rays, signals, sound, ultraviolet light, X-rays

EVOLVE

(1)   undergo development or evolution

(2)   change or gain through experience

(2) Sandra evolved from an average code writer into a top programmer over years of hard work and study.

(3)   work out a problem or issue

FECUNDATE

(1)   fertilize; great productivity; pollinate

FELL

(1)   cause to fall by delivering a blow or cutting; to cut down a tree

(2)   pass away rapidly

(3)   sew a seam by folding the edges

GASIFY

(1)   turn into a gas

GERMINATE

(1)   grow or sprout

(2)   produce buds or braches of an original

(1),(2) While some seeds will <u>germinate</u> for up to five or more years, most will <u>germinate</u> for only a year or two; seeds aged past these time limits that do germinate will not grow as much.

GREEN

(1)   turn or become green

GREEN LOG

(1)   cut trees that are still alive

METAMORPHOSE

(1)   change outward structure or looks

(2)   change completely the nature or appearance of something or someone

(1), (2) Firms that are global businesses usually <u>metamorphose</u> from local to regional to national organizations before going global.

MITIGATE

(1)   make less severe or harsh the seriousness or extent of some action or activity

<u>Collocates to: bad news, conflict, damage, danger, disruption, disaster, effect, harm, hazard, impact, loss, result, risk, threat, worst</u>

MORPH (also see Technology)

(1)   change shape in form

(2)   change shape and form in a computer animation

(1), (2) "A mixed approach is often the best. It's good for buildings to be able to <u>morph</u> from one use to the other." —Steven Harris

OFFSET (also see Art Forms and Painting/Printmaking)

(1) compensate for or counterbalance something

(2) make up for

(3) cause printed material to transfer or smear onto another surface

OSSIFY

(1) become bony and hard

(2) become rigid and set in a conventional or traditional pattern

SPLAY

(1) spread open or apart

(1) "Rivers and tributaries, which splay out across the eastern and central U.S., are like a tree with many branches." —Cameron McWhither, Wall Street Journal, *14 July 2012, p. A3*

(2) turn outward or move out of position

UPLIFT

(1) lift Earth's crust through different tectonic actions

(1) "Darwin and Captain Robert FitzRoy found mussel beds rotting ten feet above the waterline, indicating recent uplift." —Richard Milner, "Seeing Corals with the Eye of Reason," Natural History *118, issue 1, February 2009, p. 18–23*

(2) fill with high spirits through encouragement and motivation

6

History, Ancient and Modern: Mankind, Military, and Combat

MANKIND, GOVERNMENT, AND POLITICS

ABDICATE

(1) abandon; cede; demit; discard; relinquish; renounce; repudiate; resign; surrender (especially from a powerful position)

(1) The most famous abdication in recent history came in 1936, when Britain's Edward VIII abdicated the throne because the British establishment would not permit him to marry Wallis Simpson, an American divorcee.

(1) Napoleon, pressured to abdicate by his marshals in 1814, declared, "Why is it always Wellington?"— Jeremy Black, Military History 22, issue 3, Spring 2010, p. 66

Collocates to: duties, position, responsibilities, throne, office

ABIDE

(1) bear; continue; endure; go on being; put up with; stomach; take; tolerate

(1) "Gadhafi's government had lost all legitimacy and lied when it declared Friday it would abide by a cease-fire." —Associated Press, 2011

(1) "I am not liked as a President by the politicians in office, in the press, or in Congress. But I am content to abide the judgment the sober second thought of the people." —President Rutherford B. Hayes

(2) hold; remain; stay; stand fast; stand for

(3) await; to remain with someone; to stay

43

ABJURE

(1) disown; reject or disavow a previously held belief or view, usually under pressure or oath; renounce or turn one's back on a position once held; repudiate; formally recant; renounce; repudiate

(2) foreswear; give up one's rights under oath; profess to abandon; renounce; reject

(1),(2) Foreign-born individuals who want to become U.S. citizens must take an oath of allegiance in which they swear to absolutely and entirely renounce and abjure all allegiance and fidelity to any foreign prince, potentate, state, or sovereignty.

ABOLISH

(1) abrogate; annihilate; annul; eradicate; invalidate; negate; nullify; renounce; repeal; rescind

(2) bring an end to; cancel; close down; do away with; put an end to; stop

(1),(2) "Educate your children to self-control, to the habit of holding passion and prejudice and evil tendencies subject to an upright and reasoning will and you have done much to abolish misery from their future and crimes from society." —Benjamin Franklin

(1), (2) "The world is very different now. For man holds in his mortal hands the power to abolish all forms of human poverty and all forms of human life. And yet the same revolutionary beliefs for which our forebears fought are still at issue around the globe—the belief that the rights of man come not from the generosity of the state, but from the hand of God." —John F. Kennedy, presidential inaugural address, 20 January 1961

(1), (2) "The theory of Communism may be summed up in one sentence: Abolish all private property." —Karl Marx

Antithesis: "Abolish plutocracy if you would abolish poverty. As millionaires increase, pauperism grows; the more millionaires, the more paupers." —President Rutherford B. Hayes

ABOUND (in or with)

(1) flourish; present in large numbers; teeming with; thrive

(2) be plentiful; be fully supplied; be rich and abundant; have plenty of; proliferate

(1),(2) "Every wise, just, and mild government, by rendering the condition of its subjects easy and secure, will always abound most in people, as well as in commodities and riches."—David Hume, Scottish philosopher, historian, economist, and essayist, (1711–1776)

Antithesis: "A faithful man will abound with blessings, But he who makes haste to be rich will not go unpunished." —Bible

ABROGATE

(1) abolish; annul; do away with; get rid of; negate; nullify by authority;

(1) Do not abrogate that responsibility.

(2) the repeal of a law, treaty, or contract, either by mutual agreement or unilaterally

Collocates to: agreements, contracts, duty and honor, freedom, treaty, responsibility, rights

ACCLIMATE

(1) acclimatize; adapt; accustom yourself; adjust; become accustomed to a new environment or situation; familiarize; get used to

Collocates to: altitude, culture, climate, confinement, levels, surroundings, temperature, weather

ACCLIMATIZE

(1) acclimate; adapt; adjust; become accustomed to; get used to; familiarize

ACCRETE

(1) grow by accretion; increase in size; make larger or greater by accumulation of separate things

(1) A bureaucracy's original mission is to accrete money and power beyond the voter's intent.

(1) As newly formed planets form and accrete disk material and grow, they get into a gravitational tug-of-war with other celestial bodies.

ACCULTURATE

(1) adjust; adopt; cause (as in a society, for example) to change by the process of acculturation; change behavior to suit a new culture

(1) "As immigration grew in the late 1980s and 1990s, federal targeted assistance programs to acculturate and resettle newcomers did not keep pace with the increased need." —Sharon Keigher, "America's Most Cruel Xenophobia," Health & Social Work *22, issue 3, August 1997, p. 232–237*

ADMINISTER

(1) control; deal out; direct; dispense; furnish a benefit; give out; govern; hand out; manage; mete out; order; run; supervise; oversee a process

(1) The UN will administer the country following the abdication of the monarch.

(1) "In a free society, the state does not administer the affairs of men. It administers justice among men who conduct their own affairs." —Walter Lippman, American public intellectual, writer, reporter, and political commentator (1889–1974)

AGITATE

(1) attempt to stir up public opinion

(1) A number of Hollywood personalities attempt to agitate and bring about change, which is a job many have little or no experience in.

(1) "'Organize, agitate, educate,' must be our war cry." —Susan B. Anthony

(2) exert oneself continuously, vigorously, and even forcefully to gain an end or engage in a crusade for a certain cause or idea

(3) change the arrangement or position of

Collocates to: change, government, groups, issues, masses, movement

Repetition: "Nothing can hold Me up or agitate Me or cast a shadow on Me, come in this Human form, be certain of that." —Sir Sathya Sai Baba, Indian guru, spiritual figure, mystic, choreographer, philanthropist, and educator (1926–2011)

ALLY

(1)   affiliate; align; associate; befriend; confederate; consort; friend; helper; league; join; place in a friendly association, as by treaty; support

(1) Great Britain has <u>allied</u> itself with America in many wars and conflicts.

(2)   unite or connect in a personal relationship, as in friendship or marriage

AMERICANIZE

(1)   conform to American characteristics

(1) "Yes, <u>Americanism</u> evolves, and by all means let's change our minds when we ought to." —David Gelernter, "What Is the American Creed?" Wall Street Journal, *2 July 2012*

ANNEX

(1)   add to something; appropriate; attach; capture; invade; occupy; seize; take control; take over; unite

(1) It has the advantage of a side wing, ideal for use as a guest <u>annex</u>.

ANNIHILATE

(1)   conquer; crush; kill

(2)   demolish; destroy completely; put out of existence

(1), (2) <u>Annihilate</u> opposition rather than simply defeat it.

(3)   consider or cause to be of no importance or without effect; nullify

Parallelism: "By <u>annihilating</u> the desires, you <u>annihilate</u> the mind." —Claude Adrien Helvetius, French philosopher (1715–1771)

Vivid imagery: "Try as you will, you cannot <u>annihilate</u> that eternal relic of the human heart, love."
—Victor Hugo, French poet, novelist, and dramatist (1802–1885)

APPEASE

(1)   make peace with by giving in to unreasonable demands or threats out of weakness or stupidity

(1) The British and French governments <u>appeased</u> Hitler and allowed the Nazi occupation of the Sudetenland in Czechoslovakia in 1938 without taking any action.

(1) "The Communist threat is a global one. Its successful advance in one sector threatens the destruction of every other sector. You cannot appease or otherwise surrender to communism in Asia without simultaneously undermining our efforts to halt its advance in Europe."
—Gen. Douglas MacArthur, farewell address to U.S. Congress, Washington, D.C., 19 April 1951

(2)   overcome or allay

(3)   cause to be more favorably inclined

BACK CAST

(1)   describe something or some time in the past without having seen or experienced it; reconstruct past events on the basis of the study of events or other evidence

BALKANIZE

(1)   divide a territory into small hostile states, as happened to the Balkan states (Yugoslavia, Bulgaria, Greece, Albania, Turkey, and Romania) after World War I

(1) To balkanize refers to the political situation in the Balkans (c. 1878–1913) when the European section of the Ottoman Empire split up into small, warring nations.

BARTER

(1)   exchange; trade one thing for another

(2)   trade or exchange goods or services without using money

Antithesis: "It is a clear truth that those who every day barter away other men's liberty will soon care little for their own." —James Otis, lawyer in colonial Massachusetts, a member of the Massachusetts provincial assembly (1723–1785)

Metaphor: "Almost all of our relationships begin and most of them continue as forms of mutual exploitation, a mental or physical barter, to be terminated when one or both parties run out of goods." —W. H. Auden, American poet, dramatist, and editor (1907–1973)

BULLET VOTE

(1) cause or instigate a rapid vote or series of votes; voter selects only one candidate, despite the option to indicate a preference for other candidates

(1) If enough voters bullet vote, almost any voting system functions like a plurality voting system.

CAUCUS

(1) confer; convention; meet to select or nominate candidates or promote a policy; nominate

(1) The caucus steering group was elected.

Alliteration: "I have learned the difference between a cactus and a caucus. On a cactus, the pricks are on the outside." —Morris K. Udall, American congressman (1922–1998)

Antithesis: "A sailing ship is no democracy; you don't caucus a crew as to where you'll go anymore than you inquire when they'd like to shorten sail." —Sterling Hayden, American actor and author (1916–1986)

COERCE

(1) cause to do something by physical, moral, ethical, or intellectual pressure or necessity; force; intimidate; threaten

(1) The new CEO will not gain the support of the employees if he attempts to coerce their cooperation.

Antithesis: "A woman simply is, but a man must become. Masculinity is risky and elusive. It is achieved by a revolt from woman, and it is confirmed only by other men. Manhood coerced into sensitivity is no manhood at all." —Camille Paglia, American author, teacher, and social critic (1947–)

Repetition: "A man has to learn that he cannot command things, but that he can command himself; that he cannot coerce the wills of others, but that he can mold and master his own will: and things serve him who serves truth; people seek guidance of him who is master of himself." —James Allen, British philosophical writer (1864–1912)

COEXIST

(1)   exist peacefully together or side by side

(1) During the Cold War, the major powers determined that <u>coexistence</u> was preferable to the alternative, which could have been a nuclear holocaust.

Antithesis: "In economics, hope and faith <u>coexist</u> with great scientific pretension and also a deep desire for respectability." —John Kenneth Galbraith

Antithesis: "The present and the past <u>coexist</u>, but the past shouldn't be in flashback." —Alain Resnais, French film director (1922–)

Parallelism: "The only alternative to <u>coexistence</u> is codestruction." —Jawaharlal Nehru, Indian prime minister (1889–1964)

Repetition: "I think sometimes when children grow up, their parents grow up. Mine grew up with me. We <u>coexist</u>. I don't try to change them anymore, and I don't think they try to change me. We agree to disagree." —Katy Perry, singer

CONSPIRE

(1)   combine; commit; concur; crime; engage in plotting or enter into a conspiracy; swear together to act in unison or agreement and in secret to commit a deceitful or illegal act; make a secret agreement; plot; plan for

(1) The court was made aware of the prosecution's attempt to <u>conspire</u> to intimidate the defendant.

Metaphor: "Of all the causes which <u>conspire</u> to blind man's erring judgment, and misguide the mind; What the weak head with strongest bias rules—is pride, the never-failing vice of fools." —Alexander Pope, English poet (1688–1744)

Metaphor: "All deep, earnest thinking is but the intrepid effort of the soul to keep the open independence of her sea; while the wildest winds of heaven and earth <u>conspire</u> to cast her upon the treacherous, slavish shore." —Herman Melville, American author (1819–1891); *Moby-Dick* in eds. Hershel Parker, G. Thomas Tanselle, and Harrison Hayford, *The Writings of Herman Melville,* Vol. 6 (1988), Chapter 23

Parallelism: "Where justice is denied, where poverty is enforced, where ignorance prevails, and where any one class is made to feel that society is an organized <u>conspiracy</u> to oppress, rob and degrade them, neither persons nor property will be safe." —Fredrick Douglass

Simile: To <u>conspire</u> against one's country is *like* an act of patricide.

CRUSADE

(1)   exert oneself continuously, vigorously, and, if necessary, force to gain an end for a cause or belief

(2)   go on a crusade

Collocates to: cause, embark, launch, start, took, went

Metaphor: "Democracy is now going forth on a crusade against imperialism."
—Irving Babbitt, American academic and literary critic (1865–1923)

DERADICALIZE

(1)   cause to abandon or retreat from an extreme position in politics

*(1) "Although we cannot know whether politics will ultimately deradical-
ize violent groups, we do know that excluding them from the political
process grants them power without responsibility." —Condoleezza Rice,
"Rethinking the National Interest," Foreign Affairs 87, issue 4,
July/August 2008, p. 2–26*

DESTABILIZE

(1)   be incapable of functioning; unbalance; undermine; upset the stability or equilibrium of; subvert

*(1) "Today, the biggest shocks for emerging economies are far more
likely to be sudden shifts in capital flows, which destabilize because they
threaten sudden and unwanted currency depreciation." —Zanny Minton
Beddoes, "From EMU to AMU?" Foreign Affairs 78, issue 4, July/August
1999, p. 8–13*

*(1) An abandonment of our established allies would seriously destabilize
the world, especially the Middle East.*

Alliteration: If you wish to destroy, devastate, and damage a community, all
that needs to be done is simply to destabilize the social capital foundations.

Simile: To destabilize the family unit and expect no ramifications is like jack-
hammering a building's foundation and being surprised when it comes crash-
ing down in the first tumult.

EXILE

(1)   to be expelled from one's family, home, land, or country

(1) "One hundred years later, the Negro is still languished in the corners of American society and finds himself an exile in his own land. And so we've come here today to dramatize a shameful condition."
—Martin Luther King, "I Have a Dream," 28 August 1963

Metaphor: "We all carry within us our places of exile, our crimes, and our ravages. But our task is not to unleash them on the world; it is to fight them in ourselves and in others." —Albert Camus, French novelist, essayist, and playwright (1913–1960)

Repetition: "The Jewish people have been in exile for 2,000 years; they have lived in hundreds of countries, spoken hundreds of languages and still they kept their old language, Hebrew. They kept their Aramaic, later their Yiddish; they kept their books; they kept their faith." —Isaac Bashevis Singer, Polish-born American writer (1904–1991)

Vivid imagery: "I know that men in exile feed on hopes." —Aeschylus, Greek tragedian (525–456 B.C.); *Agamemnon*

EXTRADITE

(1)   to hand over to the authorities of another country; surrender of an alleged offender or fugitive to the state in whose territory the alleged offense was committed

(1) The U.S. will seek to extradite any who commits a crime in this country and attempts to avoid punishment by fleeing to another country.

FILL THE TREE

(1)   in the U.S. Congress, to take all available slots for amendments on legislation, to block competing amendments

FORAGE

(1)   collect; hunt or search for provisions; ravage; rove; search; wander and look for food

(1) "For the Gulf States, perhaps no forage crop of which the available seed supply is relatively abundant exceeds the velvet bean in potential value. This legume possesses also the ability to make a crop when planted relatively late." —David F. Houston, American politician

GERRYMANDER

(1) deliberately and unfairly arrange voting districts to favor one party or group, usually by those who are in power and want to preserve it

(2) divide unfairly and to one's advantage

Collocates to: correction, drawn, reestablish, redistrict, voting bloc

Antithesis: "It's the first case in which the redistricting was for a political gerrymander. It wasn't a byproduct. It was the goal." —Rolando Rios

IMPOSE

(1) assess; apply or establish authority exact; force one's self; levy; pass off; put

(1) "America has its origins in a rebellion against arbitrary and pernicious taxation, and the framers wanted to make it extremely difficult to impose or raise taxes." —David Gelernter, Wall Street Journal, *Opinion, 2 July 2012*

(1) "Wise teachers impart their knowledge; inept ones impose theirs." —Leonard Roy Frank, American human rights activist (1932–)

Antithesis: "Do not impose on others what you yourself do not desire." —Confucius, China's most famous teacher, philosopher, and political theorist (551–479 B.C.)

Antithesis: "Our universities are so determined to impose tolerance that they'll expel you for saying what you think and never notice the irony." —John Perry Barlow, American poet and essayist (1947–)

Metaphor: "He who has suffered you to impose on him knows you." —William Blake, English mystic, poet, painter, and engraver (1757–1827)

Parallelism: "If you haven't the strength to impose your own terms upon life, you must accept the terms it offers you." —T. S. Eliot, American-born English editor, playwright, poet, and critic (1888–1965)

INTERVENE

(1)   get involved through force or threat of force, to alter or hinder an action

(2)   be placed or located between other things, or extend between spaces and events

(1), (2) "And then, of course, the joint decision of the United States and NATO to intervene in Kosovo and save those victims, those refugees, those who were uprooted by a man, whom I believe that because of his crimes, should be charged with crimes against humanity. But this time, the world was not silent. This time, we do respond. This time, we intervene." —Elie Wiesel, The Perils of Indifference speech, 12 April 1999

JAWBONE

(1)   use persuasion rather than force to get someone to do what you want

(1) The U.S. has tried continually to jawbone the government of Pakistan to weed out Al-Qaida supporters within its military.

(2) "More Obamacare insanity: Sebelius' shameless attempt to jawbone insurers on costs" (headline) —Andrea Tantaros, Daily News *Staff Writer, 23 December 2010*

Simile: "Alcatraz, the federal prison with a name like the blare of a trombone, is a black molar in the jawbone of the nation's prison system." —Thomas E. Gaddis, American author (1908–1984)

KNOCK AND DRAG

(1)   go door-to-door on an election day in search of favorable voters to escort to voting stations

MUCKRAKE

(1)   search for and publicize any real or alleged corruption by public officials, business executives, or other important persons

(1) "Every good newspaper is muckraking, to some degree. It's part of our job. Where there's muck, we ought to rake it." —James P. Cannon, American Trotskyist and a leader of the Socialist Workers Party (1890–1974)

Parallelism: "We muckraked, not because we hated our world, but because we loved it. We were not hopeless, we were not cynical, we were not bitter." — Ray Stannard Baker, also known by pen name David Grayson, American journalist and author (1870–1946)

PERMIT

(1) allow; consent or give permission; countenance; let; license; tolerate

(2) make it possible through a specific action or lack of action for something to happen

Antithesis: "The pursuit of truth does not permit violence on one's opponent." —Mahatma Gandhi, Indian philosopher (1869–1948)

Metaphor: "Bring your desires down to your present means. Increase them only when your increased means permit." —Aristotle, ancient Greek philosopher, scientist, and physician (384 B.C.–22 B.C.)

Repetition: "I called for reinforcements but was informed that reinforcements were not available. I made clear that if not permitted to destroy the enemy built-up bases north of the Yalu, if not permitted to utilize the friendly Chinese Force of some 600,000 men on Formosa, if not permitted to blockade the China coast to prevent the Chinese Reds from getting succor from without, and if there were to be no hope of major reinforcements, the position of the command from the military standpoint forbade victory." —Gen. Douglas MacArthur, farewell address to the U.S. Congress, 19 April 1951

Vivid imagery: "Once you permit those who are convinced of their own superior rightness to censor and silence and suppress those who hold contrary opinions, just at that moment the citadel has been surrendered." —Archibald MacLeish, American poet and critic (1892–1982)

SANCTION

(1) use punitive measures

(2) penalty for wrongdoing

(1) Congress passed a bill to create sanctions on any country that suppressed free speech.

(3) give authority or permission to

Metaphor: "I yield to no one in my devotion to this great League of Nations, but not even for this will I destroy that smaller but older league of which my own country was the birthplace, and of which it remains the center. Beware how you so *draw tight the bonds*, how you so pile obligation on obligation and sanction on sanction, lest at last you find that you are not *living nations but dead states*." —Sir (Joseph) Austen Chamberlain, speech to the League of Nations Assembly, 9 September 1919

Antithesis: "The president has sanctioned greed at the cost of compassion."

ADVANCE

(1)   approach; boost; bring forward; cause to move forward, also in the metaphorical sense; come along; come on; elevate; encourage; further; gain; gain ground; get ahead; get along; go on; give a promotion or assign a higher position

(2)   contribute to the progress or growth or improve; make headway; march on; overture; pass on; progress; promote; raise; set ahead; upgrade

(1), (2) "So, first of all, let me assert my firm belief that the only thing we have to fear is fear itself—nameless, unreasoning, unjustified terror which paralyzes needed efforts to convert retreat into <u>advance</u>."
—President Franklin Delano Roosevelt, first presidential inaugural speech, 4 March 1933

Antithesis: "You can't say civilizations don't <u>advance</u> … in every war, they kill you in a new way." —Mark Twain

Metaphor: "The difficulties you meet will resolve themselves as you <u>advance</u>. Proceed, and light will dawn, and shine with increasing clearness on your path." —Jim Rohn, American speaker and author (1930–2009)

Parallelism: "Why should we be frightened? No people who have ever lived on this earth have fought harder, paid a higher price for freedom, or done more to <u>advance</u> the dignity of man than the living Americans, those Americans living in this land today." —President Ronald Reagan (1911–2004)

Simile: "Learning is *like* rowing upstream; not to <u>advance</u> is to drop back." —ancient Chinese proverb

ATTACK

(1)   approach; assail; attempt to launch an assault; begin to injure someone; blast; fire; flank; onrush; onset; set upon; snipe

(2)   set to work on; take the initiative and go on the offensive

Alliteration: "Men rise from one ambition to another: first, they seek to secure themselves against <u>attack</u>, and then they <u>attack</u> others." —Niccolo Machiavelli, Italian writer and statesman, Florentine patriot, and author of "The Prince" (1469–1527)

Antithesis: "Invincibility lies in the defense; the possibility of victory in the <u>attack</u>." —Sun Tzu, Chinese general and author (b. 500 B.C.)

Metaphor: "Yesterday, December 7th, 1941—a date which will live in infamy—the United States of America was suddenly and deliberately <u>attacked</u> by naval and air forces of the Empire of Japan." —President Franklin Roosevelt, address to the nation, 8 December 1941

Repetition: "Nobody ever defended anything successfully; there is only <u>attack</u> and <u>attack</u> and <u>attack</u> some more." —Gen. George S. Patton, American general in World War I and World War II (1885–1945)

Repetition: "Yesterday, the Japanese government also launched an <u>attack</u> against Malaya. Last night, Japanese forces <u>attacked</u> Hong Kong. Last night, Japanese forces <u>attacked</u> Guam. Last night, Japanese forces <u>attacked</u> the Philippine Islands. Last night, the Japanese <u>attacked</u> Wake Island. And this morning, the Japanese <u>attacked</u> Midway Island." —President Franklin Roosevelt, address to the nation, 8 December 1941

Simile: <u>Attack</u> *as* viciously as a lioness attacking a gazelle in search of a meal for her cubs.

BATTLE

(1)   combat; competition; duel; encounter; fight; fracas; fray; melee; skirmish; wage a fight against

(1)   "<u>Battle</u> is the most magnificent competition in which a human being can indulge. It brings out all that is best; it removes all that is base. All men are afraid in <u>battle</u>. The coward is the one who lets his fear overcome his sense of duty. Duty is the essence of manhood." —Gen. George Patton

(1)   "It is impossible to win the race unless you venture to run, impossible to win the victory unless you dare to <u>battle</u>." —Richard M. DeVoos, American businessman, cofounder of Amway (1926–)

Antithesis: "A <u>battle</u> lost or won is easily described, understood, and appreciated, but the moral growth of a great nation requires reflection, as well as observation, to appreciate it." —Frederick Douglass

Antithesis: "The general who wins the <u>battle</u> makes many calculations in his temple before the battle is fought. The general who loses makes but few calculations beforehand." —Sun Tzu, Chinese general

Metaphor: "Humanity has won its <u>battle</u>. Liberty now has a country." —Marquis de Lafayette

Parallelism: "The <u>battle</u> of life is, in most cases, fought uphill; and to win it without a struggle were perhaps to win it without honor. If there were no difficulties there would be no success; if there were nothing to struggle for, there would be nothing to be achieved." —Samuel Smiles, Scottish author and reformer (1812–1904)

Repetition: "I believe in the battle—whether it's the battle of a campaign or the battle of this office, which is a continuing battle." —President Richard M. Nixon

Simile: "As a man sows, shall he reap. And I know that talk is cheap. But the heat of the battle is *as sweet as the victory*." —Bob Marley

Vivid imagery: "A lost battle is a battle one thinks one has lost." —Jean-Paul Sartre, French existentialist philosopher, playwright, novelist, screenwriter, and political activist (1905–1980)

BESIEGE

(1) beleaguer; beset; blockade; grasp without letting go; harass; harry; hound; importune; lay siege to; pester; plague; surround

Alliteration: We are beleaguered, beset, and besieged by these enemies.

Metaphor: "Though an army besiege me, my heart will not fear; though war break out against me, even then will I be confident." —Bible

BOMBARD

(1) attack; barrage; bomb; open fire on; pile on; hit with heavy forces

(1) Our brains are continuously bombarded with enormous amounts of information from each of the senses.

BUSHWHACK

(1) ambush; attack; defeat, especially by surprise; lie in wait; lurk

(1) The bushwhack was a favorite tactic of outlaws of the old West.

(1) "During the Civil War, the area became a refuge for service-dodging Texans, and gangs of bushwhackers, as they were called, hid in its vastness. Conscript details of Confederate Army hunted the fugitives, and occasional skirmishes resulted." —Administration in the State of Texas, "U.S. Public Relief Program (1935–1943)," Texas: A Guide to the Lone Star State (The WPA Guide to Texas), *Hastings House, 1940, p. 410*

CAMPAIGN

(1) agitate; battle; canvass; cause; crusade; engage; drive; effort; fight; hold an operation; participate; press; push; struggle

Metaphor: "I have tried to talk about the issues in this campaign … and this has sometimes been a lonely road, because I never meet anybody coming the other way." —Adlai E. Stevenson, American politician (1900–1965)

Metaphor: "Christianity is the story of how the rightful King has landed, you might say in disguise, and is calling us all to take part in His great campaign of sabotage." —C. S. Lewis, British scholar and novelist (1898–1963)

Simile: "To campaign against colonialism is *like* barking up a tree that has already been cut down." —Andrew Cohen, American philosopher and visionary (1955–)

CANNONADE

(1) barrage; bombardment; onslaught; outpouring of words or blows; volley

(1) After the British ship had fired a single 64-pound cannonade, the French vessel surrendered, fearing it would be outgunned.

CAPTAIN

(1) be in command; lead; command; control; manage something; skipper

Antithesis: If the highest aim of a captain were to preserve his ship, he would keep it in port forever." —St. Thomas Aquinas, scholastic philosopher and theologian (1225–1274)

Antithesis: "I had rather have a plain, russet-coated Captain, that knows what he fights for, and loves what he knows, than that which you call a Gentle-man and is nothing else." —Oliver Cromwell, English military and political leader and later Lord Protector of the Commonwealth of England (1599–1658)

Simile: "For a politician to complain about the press is *like* a ship's captain complaining about the sea." —Enoch Powell

CIRCUMNAVIGATE

(1) around but not through; skirt; pass

(1) Tourists can fairly easily circumnavigate the World Trade Center rebuilding project.

CIRCUMVALLATE

(1) surround with or use as a rampart or fortification

CONSCRIPT

(1) compulsory enrollment; draft; sign-up

(1) Conscript troops and too few elite forces do not make a good fighting force.

(1) "During the Civil War, the area became a refuge for service-dodging Texans, and gangs of bushwhackers, as they were called, hid in its vastness. Conscript details of Confederate Army hunted the fugitives, and occasional skirmishes resulted." —Administration in the State of Texas, "U.S. Public Relief Program (1935–1943)," Texas: A Guide to the Lone Star State (The WPA Guide to Texas), *Hastings House, 1940, p. 410*

DEPOPULATE

(1) reduce the population by violence or disease

DERACINATE

(1) dig up; eradicate; isolate; remove or separate from native or comfortable environment; uproot; rip up

DRAGOON

(1) coerce or force one into doing something; compel by coercion, threats, or crude means

(1) During the American Revolution, the British forces would dragoon colonists for service.

(1) During World War II, the Allies conducted a post-Normandy landing called Operation Dragoon.

DRAW FIRE

(1) attract the fire of others; expose oneself to danger for the sake of others

(1) Don't draw fire; it irritates the people around. —Bumper sticker

DUEL

(1) fence; fight; oppose; resist

(1) I had never heard of a man in his right mind going out to fight a duel without first making his will.

ENFILADE

(1)   attack the flank of one's enemies; direct gunfire to the flank

(2)   assault or attack an enemy on their flank

(1), (2) During World War I, the combatants made extensive use of trenches because they helped to contain explosions and helped prevent enfilade firing in the event the enemy gain control of any part of them.

LAUNCH

(1)   begin with vigor; establish; mount; plunge; set in motion; propel by force

(1) "Yesterday, the Japanese government also launched an attack against Malaya. Last night, Japanese forces attacked Hong Kong. Last night, Japanese forces attacked Guam. Last night, Japanese forces attacked the Philippine Islands. Last night, the Japanese attacked Wake Island. And this morning, the Japanese attacked Midway Island."
—President Franklin Roosevelt, address to the nation, 8 December 1941

(1) "You will launch many projects but have time to finish only a few. So think, plan, develop, launch, and tap good people to be responsible. Give them authority and hold them accountable. Trying to do too much yourself creates a bottleneck." —Donald Rumsfeld, American Secretary of Defense

Metaphor: "The small force that it takes to launch a boat into the stream should not be confused with the force of the stream that carries it along: but this confusion appears in nearly all biographies." —Friedrich Nietzsche, German classical scholar and philosopher (1844–1900)

Parallelism: "You must live in the present, launch yourself on every wave, find your eternity in each moment. Fools stand on their island opportunities and look toward another land. There is no other land, there is no other life but this." —Henry David Thoreau, American essayist, poet, and philosopher (1817–1862)

PLAN

(1)   be after; contrive; design; program; project

(1) "To achieve great things, two things are needed; a plan and not quite enough time." —Leonard Bernstein, American conductor, composer, and pianist (1918–1990)

Alliteration: "In preparing for battle, I have always found that plans are useless, but planning is indispensable." —Gen. Dwight D. Eisenhower

Alliteration: "Four steps to achievement: Plan purposefully. Prepare prayer-fully. Proceed positively. Pursue persistently." —William Arthur Ward, American scholar, author, editor, pastor, and teacher

Metaphor: "Do you wish to rise? Begin by descending. You plan a tower that will pierce the clouds? Lay first the foundation of humility." —Saint Augustine

Parallelism: "To accomplish great things, we must not only act, but also dream; not only plan, but also believe." —Anatole France, French poet, journalist, and novelist (1844–1924)

SABER RATTLE

(1)   flamboyant display of military power

(2)   threat or implied threat to use military force

   (1), (2) The Iranian military exercises in the Straits of Hormuz are a way for their leaders to saber rattle.

TOMAHAWK

(1)   attack, beat, cut, or hit with a tomahawk; chop as with a tomahawk

7

Human Life and the Development of Human Life: Health and Disease, Types of Human Behavior and Experience, Nature, and Climate

HEALTH AND DISEASE

AMPUTATE

(1)   cut off; prune; remove by cutting

(1)   "So someday in the near future hopefully rather than having a foot or a leg amputated, we'll just give you an injection of the cells and restore the blood flow. We've also created entire tubes of red blood cells from scratch in the laboratory. So there are a lot of exciting things in the pipeline."
—Robert Lanza, American doctor of medicine and scientist (1956–)

ANESTHETIZE

(1)   deaden; freeze; subject one to anesthesia; immobilize one; numb; put out or under; sedate

Metaphor: "Egotism is the <u>anesthetic</u> that dulls the pain of stupidity." —Frank Leahy, football coach of the University of Notre Dame (1908–1973)

Simile: "Life *is* pain and the enjoyment of love *is* an <u>anesthetic</u>." —Cesare Pavese, Italian poet, critic, novelist, and translator (1908–1950)

Antithesis: "Each wrong act brings with it its own <u>anesthetic</u>, dulling the conscience and blinding it against further light, and sometimes for years." —Rose McCaulay, English writer (1881–1958)

AURALIZE

(1)   hear mentally; imagine the sound of something

ETIOLATE (ē'tē ə lāt')

(1)   cause to become pale, unhealthy, or weak; appear sickly

   *(1) "But we heard something somewhere, crying. They were <u>etiolate</u> cries
   of anguish and excruciation beyond human comprehending, endurance,
   or pity. We lay around in the valley for a few days." —Tanith Lee, "In the
   City of Dead Night,"* Fantasy & Science Fiction *103, issue 4/5, 1992,
   p. 198*

(2)   deprive of strength; weaken

(3)   blanch or bleach by depriving of sunlight

GORMANDIZE

(1)   binge; chow down; eat gluttonously or devour ravenously; englut; feed;
      glutton; gorge; greedily overindulge; pig out; satiate; scarf out; swallow

MACERATE

(1)   separate into constituents by soaking

(2)   soften, usually after soaking in a liquid

(3)   cause to grow thin or weak; waste away by or as if by excessive fasting

PALLIATE

(1)   treat someone so that symptoms subside even though he or she still has
      the disorder or disease

   *(1) "The medications that we have help to <u>palliate</u> the impulsivity and
   the mood disorder, the mood disregulation. The psychotherapies are in no
   way curative; they are primarily supportive." —Patrick Perry,
   "Personality Disorders: Coping with the Borderline,"* Saturday Evening
   Post *269, issue 4, July/August 1997, p. 44–84*

ROBOTRIP

(1)   use over-the-counter cough syrup for its narcotic effects

NEGATIVE OR UNPLEASANT HUMAN BEHAVIOR

ABETTED

(1) advocate; aid; approve; assist; back; back up; encourage; espouse; foment; help incite; put up to; sanction; support; urge (especially in wrongdoing)

(1) The trend of larger classes makes for disorder, but it is abetted by another trend, and that is teachers losing control of their students.

Metaphor: "Abetted by corrupt analysts, patients who have nothing better to do with their lives often use the psychoanalytic situation to transform insignificant childhood hurts into private shrines at which they worship unceasingly the enormity of the offenses committed against them. This solution is immensely flattering to the patients—as are all forms of unmerited self-aggrandizement; it is immensely profitable for the analysts—as are all forms pandering to people's vanity; and it is often immensely unpleasant for nearly everyone else in the patient's life." —Thomas Szasz, psychiatrist and academic (1920–2012)

ABSQUATULATE (ăb- skwŏch´ĕ-lāt)

(1) decamp; run off or run away; flee; escape; hurry off; leave in a hurry

(1) If you rent a stable horse, it can easily absquatulate if you dismount.

(2) abscond

(3) argue

ACERBATE

(1) annoy or vex; irritate; make something taste bitter or sour

(1) Alex knew how passionate and agitated the crowd was, so rather than acerbate them further, he tempered his remarks.

(1) His childlike actions acerbate his fellow classmates and make it hard to carry on a meaningful conversation.

ADDLE

(1) befuddle; confuse; make confused; be mentally uncertain

(1) "In following the separate and shared paths of the novel's principal characters from childhood into middle age, Ms. Mitchell and company are out to beguile and addle all the senses." —Ben Brantley, "Six Lives Ebb and Flow, Interconnected and Alone," New York Times, 2008

(2)   muddle

(3)   rot

Metaphor: "Speech is often barren; but silence also does not necessarily brood over a full nest. Your still fowl, blinking at you without remark, may all the while be sitting on one <u>addled</u> egg; and when it takes to crackling will have nothing to announce but that added delusion." —George Eliot (Mary Ann Evans), British novelist; *Felix Holt*

Simile: "I am not like that. I pay rent, am <u>addled</u> by illegible landlords, run, if robbers call." —Gwendolyn Brooks, American poet (1917–2000)

ADULTERATE

(1)   commit; contaminate; corrupt; debase; dope; impure; infect; pollute; ruin; taint

    (1)   "The vast majority of imported mixto is by established companies like Cuervo and Sauza, and we have no doubt that their product is genuine. But some of the others <u>adulterate</u> it and even use silly, offensive brand names that make Mexico look ridiculous." —Robert Collier, "Tequila Temptation; It's a National Success Story, an Authentically Mexican Symbol," San Francisco Chronicle, 19 October 1997

Metaphor: "JUSTICE, n. A commodity which is a more or less <u>adulterated</u> condition the State sells to the citizen as a reward for his allegiance, taxes, and personal service." —Ambrose Bierce, American writer, journalist, and editor (1842–1914)

Simile: "The test of friendship is assistance in adversity, and that too, unconditional assistance. Co-operation which needs consideration is a commercial contract and not friendship. Conditional co-operation is like <u>adulterated</u> cement which does not bind." —Mohandas Gandhi

AIRSHIP

(1)   steal or abscond with money collected from newspaper dealers

APOSTATIZE

(1)   renounce totally a religious belief once professed; forsake one's church, the faith or principles once held, or the party to which one has previously adhered; abandon one's beliefs or allegiances; defect; renounce; reject; tergiversate

Metaphor: "Brethren, if I were to tell you all I know of the kingdom of God, I do know that you would rise up and kill me. Don't tell me anything that I can't bear, for I don't want to <u>apostatize</u>." —Joseph Smith

ARROGATE (ar'ro gāt')

(1) assume; ascribe; baseless; claim as own; presumptions; take power that is not yours; claim; lay claim to; appropriate; misappropriate; assume; take over; demand; annex

(1) I won't arrogate to teach you about life.

Alliteration: He will arrogate, assume, and ascribe such powers to himself.

ASPENIZE

(1) become, or cause to become, tourist oriented, especially in such a way as to grow unaffordable or unlivable for workers or native residents of the town, city, or region

(1) The term aspenize derives from Aspen, Colorado, a tourist city in the United States.

(1) "People say they don't want to aspenize the county, pricing our workers and the natives out." —Kevin McCullen, Rocky Mountain News, *21 March 1993*

ASPERSE

(1) attack; insult; libel; slander

(1) A poet can asperse anything by a clever and creative simile.

ASSAIL

(1) attack; assault; beat; beset; lay into; overcome; overwhelm; pugnacious; rail; sally; set about

(1) "Clinton's missteps handed Republicans a major chance to regain the high ground on the civil rights debate. We needed just three things: rhetoric worthy of the moment; actions consistent with the rhetoric; and a Big Tent that would let us assail prejudices without creating new class frictions." Tony Snow, "The Race Card," The New Republic *207, issue 25, 14 December 1992, p. 17–20*

(2) attack verbally; berate; criticize

(3) censure; be sanctimonious

Antithesis: "In all my writings, my aim has been to spare sinners and assail sin." —Marcus Aurelius, Roman Emperor from 161 to 180 CE, (121 CE–180 CE)

Metaphor: "There mark what ills the scholar's life assail, toil, envy, want, and patron." —Samuel Johnson (1709–1784)

AWFULIZE

(1)   imagine or predict the worst circumstances or outcome

(1) Too many people tend to moralize and <u>awfulize</u> their own faults and shortcomings.

BIKE-WACK

(1)   ride a bicycle on rough terrain without paths

(1) The mountain we raced down was overgrown and strewn with rocks, requiring us to <u>bike-wack</u>.

BLOVIATE

(1)   braggadocio; be a charlatan; be a coxcomb; hubris; speak pompously

Metaphor: "Warren G. Harding was the person who invented the word <u>bloviate</u> and was the only man, woman or child who wrote a simple declarative sentence with seven grammatical errors." —e. e. Cummings

BONK

(1)   in bicycling, to become exhausted; also bonk out

BREAK THE TON (brāk-the-tŭn)

(1)   exceed and sustain 100 miles per hour in a street muscle car

(1) "When I was a kid, we all drove muscle cars with enormous hemis; the term <u>'breakin' the ton'</u> was popular slang." —Gregg, wwwslkword.com blog

BUSTLE

(1)   move or cause to move energetically or busily, seemingly without plan or direction

(1) "The <u>bustle</u> in a house the morning after death is solemnest of industries enacted upon earth, The sweeping up the heart, and putting love away we shall not want to use again until eternity." —Emily Dickinson, American poet (1830–1886)

Antithesis: "If a man knew anything, he would sit in a corner and be modest; but he is such an ignorant peacock, that he goes <u>bustling</u> up and down, and hits on extraordinary discoveries." —Ralph Waldo Emerson

Parallelism: We <u>bustle</u> through the day, we <u>bustle</u> through events, we <u>bustle</u> through life.

COLLUDE

(1)   act secretly; be in cahoots with; connive; conspire; cooperate; act cunningly; deceive; defraud; plan; plot; scheme

(1) "The involvement of the broader groups will ensure that the G-2 does not <u>collude</u> against the rest of the world and promote its own interests at everyone else's expense." —Author, "America and Europe: Clash of the Titans," Foreign Affairs 78, issue 2, March/April 1999, p. 20–34

(1) The government must listen to the families of people injured by employer negligence, not <u>collude</u> with the business world.

Alliteration: We will <u>c</u>unningly <u>c</u>ollude, <u>c</u>onnive, <u>c</u>onspire, and scheme to win a victory for freedom.

Alliteration: They <u>c</u>olluded, <u>c</u>onnived, <u>c</u>onspired, were <u>c</u>ounseled by, and were in <u>c</u>ahoots with those charlatans who would <u>c</u>avil and avoid <u>c</u>onfronting the charade of <u>c</u>harter reform.

COMMIT

(1)   engage in or perform an act upon

(2)   cause to be admitted

(3)   confer trust upon

Antithesis: "It is most pleasant to <u>commit</u> a just action which is disagreeable to someone whom one does not like." —Victor Hugo, French poet, novelist, and playwright (1802–1885); *L'Homme Qui Rit*

Antithesis: "I don't like to <u>commit</u> myself about heaven and hell—you see, I have friends in both places." —Mark Twain

Metaphor: "The achievement of your goal is assured the moment you <u>commit</u> yourself to it." —Mack R. Douglas, American author

CONDESCEND

(1)   deign; stoop to a lower level in an offensive way; patronize; vouchsafe

(1) She insulted me, but I did not <u>condescend</u> to reply.

(1) "Don't be <u>condescending</u> to unskilled labor. Try it for a half a day first." —Brooks Atkinson, American journalist and critic (1894–1984)

Antithesis: "Mind not high things, but <u>condescend</u> to men of low estate. Be not wise in your own conceits. Recompense to no man evil for evil. Provide things honest in the sight of all men. If it be possible, as much as lieth in you, live peaceably with all men. Dearly beloved, avenge not yourselves, but rather give place unto wrath: for it is written, 'Vengeance is mine; I will repay, saith the Lord.'" —Bible (Romans 12:16–19)

Antithesis: "Fortune has rarely condescended to be the companion of genius." —Isaac Disraeli, British writer (1766–1848)

Repetition: "Rain is grace; rain is the sky condescending to the earth; without rain, there would be no life." —John Updike, American writer (1932–2009)

CONTAMINATE

(1) befoul; corrupt; defile; foul; infect; make impure; poison; pollute; sully; taint

Metaphor: "Shall we now contaminate our fingers with base bribes, and sell the mighty space of our large honors for so much trash as may be grasped thus? I'd rather be a dog and bay at the moon than be such a Roman." — William Shakespeare

Simile: "Images contaminate us *like* viruses." —Paul Virilio, French cultural theorist and urbanist (1932–)

Simile: "A man who is free is like a mangy sheep in a herd. He will contaminate my entire kingdom and ruin my work." —Jean-Paul Sartre, French novelist, philosopher, dramatist, and political activist (1905–1980); King Aegistheus in *The Flies,* Act 2

CONTEMN

(1) despise; disdain; treat with scorn; querulous

(1) "A good number of writers specifically urged their readers not to despise, contemn, or use unmannerly speech or behavior towards the aged." —Dallet Hemphill, "Age Relations and the Social Order in Early New England: The Evidence from Manners," Journal of Social History *28, issue 2, Winter 1994, p. 271*

DENIGRATE

(1) attack; belittle; criticize; defame; disparage; downgrade; condemn; humiliate; lessen the significance or importance of; vilify

(1) "Milton Friedman argued, state experts implementing abstract ideals about satisfying human needs are merely blundering about in the dark.... Nothing here, of course, denigrates, the essential role of the state in providing the infrastructure of law and justice (not to mention defense) on which freedom in all its forms rests." —Kenneth Minogue, "The Death and Life of Liberal Economics," Wall Street Journal *27–28 October 2012*

Alliteration: "It is a shame to misuse our beautiful language to denigrate, defame, or disparage another individual."

Vivid Imagery: "Men are not the enemy, but the fellow victims. The real enemy is women's denigration of themselves." —Betty Friedan

Collocates to: ideas, demean, importance, mean, others, religion, tends

DESPOIL

(1) damage; deface; defile; overexploit; pillage; plunder; ravage; rob; ruin; steal; spoil; wreck; vandalize

(1) "Critics, including the Sonoma County Board of Supervisors, say the tribe's plans to build 'Rancho San Pablo' would despoil the natural beauty of the area—one of the Bay Area's last large undeveloped bayside vistas." —Jim Doyle, "Pomo Indians Plan Housing Tract on San Pablo Bay Land," San Francisco Chronicle, 15 January 1996

(1) "Aristotle said: 'Men come together in cities in order to live, but they remain together in order to live the good life.' It is harder and harder to live the good life in American cities today. The catalog of ills is long: there is the decay of the centers and the despoiling of the suburbs." President Lyndon Baines Johnson, *The Great Society Speech, Ann Arbor, Mich. 22 May 1964*

Collocates to: environment, lands, natural beauty, open space, parklands, wetlands, wilderness

DIDDLE

(1) dawdle; swindle

(1) Since the 1930s, the U.S. Congress has been able to diddle around with the income tax law so that almost no one can really understand it.

(2) be idle, indolent

(3) move back and forth in a jerky fashion

(4) (slang) masturbate or have sex

Alliteration: "God whom we see not, is: and God, who is not, we see; fiddle, we know, is diddle: and diddle, we take it, is dee." —A. C. Swinburne, British poet and critic (1837–1909); *The Heptalogia*

Parallelism: "On the contrary, everyone diddles, cheats, and frustrates everyone else, and is diddled, cheated, and frustrated in return." —Unknown

DILLYDALLY (slang)

(1)   dawdle; dither; falter; be indecisive; loiter; vacillate

      (1) Hurry up! Don't <u>dillydally</u>; we are in a hurry.

DISAFFECT

(1)   agitate; alienate; antagonize; discompose; dislike someone or something; disquiet; disturb; disunify; disunite; divide; estrange; be hostile or unsympathetic; repel; upset; wean; make distant

      (1) The strategy of colonial powers was to <u>disaffect</u> potential resistance leaders from the local native population.

      (1) "Affection cannot be manufactured or regulated by law. If one has no affection for a person or a system, one should be free to give the fullest expression to his <u>disaffection</u>, so long as he does not contemplate, promote, or incite to violence." —Mahatma Gandhi

Alliteration: The result of the party's actions were to <u>disaffect</u>, <u>d</u>isquiet, <u>d</u>isturb, <u>d</u>ivide, and create <u>d</u>isunity when it could be least afforded.

DISAVOW

(1)   deny knowledge or approval of; disclaim; disassociate; disown; refuse to acknowledge or accept; recant; reject; renounce; repudiate; turn your back on; wash one's hands of

      (1) The board of directors <u>disavowed</u> the actions of the CEO.

Antithesis: "One may <u>disavow</u> and disclaim vices that surprise us, and whereto our passions transport us; but those which by long habits are rooted in a strong and powerful will are not subject to contradiction. Repentance is but a denying of our will, and an opposition of our fantasies." —Michel Eyquem de Montaigne, French Renaissance writer (1533–1592)

DISCOMBOBULATE

(1)   bedevil; befuddle; confuse; disconcert; disrupt thinking; frustrate; upset the composure of someone

      (1) As a result of all the problems and issues he faced, his thinking had become <u>discombobulated</u>.

(2)   confuse or disconcert; frustrate; upset

      (2) "The imagery of the writer's helps to demonstrate Houdini's ability to <u>discombobulate</u> rational thought, even after a century." —Edward Rothstein, "Upside-Down King as Art Muse," New York Times, 28 October 2010

DISCOMFIT

(1)   confuse; disconcert; deject; foil; frustrate the plans of someone; inconvenience; thwart

(1) Well, they can continue debating, but I am afraid that they do not discomfit me in the least.

DISCONCERT

(1)   abash; embarrass; disappoint; displease; distress; frustrate; grieve; make uncomfortable; offend; sadden; trouble

(1) Her unusual defense strategy seemed to disconcert the prosecution team.

DISCREDIT

(1)   debunk; disbelieve; disgrace; expose; knock out the bottom; puncture; refuse credence to; refute; reject as untrue; shoot down; shoot full of holes

Antithesis: "A polite enemy is just as difficult to discredit, as a rude friend is to protect." —Bryant H. McGill, American author, speaker, and activist (1969–)

Antithesis: "Contrary to the vulgar belief that men are motivated primarily by materialistic considerations, we now see the capitalist system being discredited and destroyed all over the world, even though this system has given men the greatest material comforts." —Ayn Rand, Russian-American novelist, philosopher, playwright, and novelist (1905–1982)

Parallelism: "Until the philosophy which holds one race superior and another inferior is finally and permanently discredited and abandoned ... Everything is war. *Me say war.* That until there are no longer first class and second class citizens of any nation ... Until the color of a man's skin is of no more significance than the color of his eyes, *me say war.* That until the basic human rights are equally guaranteed to all without regard to race, *me say war!* —Bob Marley, Jamaican singer-songwriter (1945–1981)

DISPARAGE

(1)   belittle; be derisive; be caustic or disputatious; think of something as small or insignificant; lower in esteem or discredit; underestimate

(1) A frequent tactic of environmental zealots is to disparage the results of scientific research that disagrees with their ideology.

Metaphor: "To <u>disparage</u> the dictate of reason is equivalent to contemning the command of God." —Saint Thomas Aquinas

Vivid Imagery: "People <u>disparage</u> knowing and the intellectual life, and urge doing. I am content with knowing, if only I could know." —Ralph Waldo Emerson

EQUIVOCATE

(1) ambiguous; evasive; hedge; palter; prevaricate; pussyfoot; prevaricate; quibble; shuffle; waffle; mince words

(2) use equivocal terms or language in order to be decisive, mislead, hedge, or otherwise be deliberately ambiguous

(1), (2) It is not a sound strategy for a witness to <u>equivocate</u> before a grand jury.

Metaphor: "There is something suspicious about music, gentlemen. I insist that she is, by her nature, equivocal. I shall not be going too far in saying at once that she is politically suspect." —Thomas Mann, German novelist, short story writer, social critic, philanthropist, and essayist (1875–1955)

Repetition: "I am in earnest—I will not <u>equivocate</u>—I *will not excuse*—I *will not retreat* a single inch—and *I will be heard!*" —William Lloyd Garrison, U.S. abolitionist (1805–1879)

EXACERBATE *(eg zas'ər bāt')*

(1) aggravate; annoy; bilious; be contentious; embitter; exasperate; intensify; irate; make more bitter or severe; be cantankerous; worsen an already bad or difficult situation or condition

<u>Collocates to: conflicts, differences, difficulties, dilemmas, discrimination, fears, feelings, issues, injustices, problems, situations, tendencies, threats, violence</u>

Antithesis: "By speaking, by thinking, we undertake to clarify things, and that forces us to <u>exacerbate</u> them, dislocate them, schematize them. Every concept is in itself an exaggeration." —Jose Ortega y Gasset, Spanish philosopher and humanist (1883–1955)

EXCOGITATE (îk-skōj' i-tāt')

(1)   deride; devise; discover; disparage; knock; ridicule

(1)   "Philosophers have speculated on the question of God for thousands of years; the scientist must stop to observe and start to excogitate."

EXCORIATE (ek skôr'e āt')

(1)   denounce harshly

(1)   President Bush's advisors encouraged him to excoriate Congress over their inaction on the education bill.

(2)   take action that makes a situation worse; aggravate something further

(3)   abrade; abuse; assail; scrape, scratch or rub the skin off; chafe; flay

EXECRATE (also see Religion, Ethics and Morality)

(1)   curse or call evil down upon

(1)   "He was the very coin of evil, with the face and bearing of a beast— malignancy made flesh, affecting them like a cold hand upon the heart. To hear him execrate God turned their bowels to ice. To see him was to look on leprosy. And so Hyde lived, unregenerate, cursing God and Henry Jekyll—God for having given Jekyll Me, Jekyll for giving life to Hyde." — Normal Lock, "The Monster in Winter," New England Review 28, issue 3, 2007, p. 163

(2)   hate; use profane language; regard with extreme dislike; swear; use Caperlash

(3)   speak abusively of; contemptuous of; denounce scathingly

(4)   abhor; detest; loathe

Parallelism: "For thus saith the Lord of hosts, the God of Israel; As mine anger and my fury hath been poured forth upon the inhabitants of Jerusalem; so shall my fury be poured forth upon you, when ye shall enter into Egypt: and ye shall be an execration, and an astonishment, and a curse, and a reproach; and ye shall see this place no more." —Bible

FACEBRAG

(1)   brag excessively and spout off about yourself on Facebook

FLEER

(1)   be bellicose; deride; jeer; laugh imprudently; mock; ridicule; scorn derisively; sneer

> *(1)   Diane fleered her opponent in the election.*

FLUMMOX

(1)   amaze; bedraggle; bewilder; confound; confuse; cause one to be perplexed; dumbfound; gravel; make doubtful; make uncertain; nonplus

> *(1)   Some new digital applications can flummox the savviest mobile users.*

Alliteration: "Flummoxed by Failure or Focused," Ken Bain, *Wall Street Journal,* 14 July 2012

FOIST

(1)   impose an unwelcome person or thing on someone

> *(1)   "Can advertising foist an inferior product on the consumer? Bitter experience has taught me that it cannot. On those rare occasions when I have advertised products which consumer tests have found inferior to other products in the same field, the results have been disastrous."*
> *—David Ogilvy, top British advertising executive (1911–1999)*

FORMICATE

(1)   feel a crawling, teeming sensation; overflow with some repugnant sensation

FREEBALL

(1)   not wear underpants (beneath clothing); go commando

> *(1)   "Call it free-balling, California casual, alfresco, or the much-preferred "going commando." Unless that sundress is super susceptible to breeze, super short, or you're super drunk, no one will know the difference." —Rebekah Gleaves,* Memphis Flyer, *26 June 2004*

FULMINATE

(1)   explode; expel something; turn against something

GAINSAY (gān'sā')

(1) deny; dispute; contradict; refuse to believe or grant the truth of something

(1) He was a founding member of the religion, yet the church leaders wanted him to gainsay his faith.

GANK

(1) cheat; flimflam; honeyfuggle; rob, rip off, or con (someone); be a snollygoster

(1) "When you see ah sucker, stick out yo belly and put on a sad face. Then you be like, Sir (or Madame), could you spare me a quarter for sumpin to eat? You can gank a few. And you can pull a big draw if you can find a whole gang of suckers from the same office all bunched up together." —Jeffery Renard Allen, "Holding Pattern," Literary Review 46, Summer 2003

GASCONADE

(1) blatherskite; be brazen; use extravagantly boastful talk; be a barbermonger; be imperious

GIBE (jīb) (also see Human Behavior and Experience, Positive Behavior)

(1) heckle; jeer; laugh at with contempt and derision; mock; scoff; taunt

(2) be compatible, similar, or consistent

GIFT DEBT

(1) negative position when someone has given you a gift and you have no gift to give in return

GLOZE

(1) explain away; fawn; flatter; gloss over

(2) color to hide the original; give a deceptively attractive appearance

GORGONIZE (gôr'gən īz')

(1) paralyze or mesmerize with one's looks or personality; petrify or stupefy with a look

HACKNEY

(1) be a blooter; be doltish and a doofus; make commonplace or trite; be a plonker; stale; insipid; scurrilous

HARANGUE

(1) accost; be bellicose; berate or yell at someone or something; go on a loud, blustering rant

(1) Under the scathing criticism of the opposition, the pent-up fury of the original speaker vented itself into a fiery harangue.

HECTOR

(1) bait; bully; heckle; intimidate; push around; swagger; treat with insolence; vituperative

(1) Political debates used to be opportunities for voters to learn the candidates' views on issues, but now the debate time seems to be spent seeing who can heckle and hector their opponent more.

HIBERDATE

(1) ignore one's old friends and acquaintances when dating a new person

HIBERGAME

(1) spend all day gaming, without eating, socializing, or doing anything that requires one to leave the game

INTERPOSE

(1) aggressive; arbitrate; insert; intercept; interfere; intermediate; meddle; mediate; unsolicited opinion; offer assistance or presence; put between

(1) "Finish each day before you begin the next, and interpose a solid wall of sleep between the two. This you cannot do without temperance."
—Ralph Waldo Emerson, American poet, lecturer, and essayist
(1803–1882)

INVEIGLE (in vā'gəl)

(1) convince or persuade someone through trickery, deception, dishonesty, or flattery

(1) Former President Clinton had a scheme to inveigle several big insurance firms to cover his legal costs of impeachment.

JUMP UGLY

(1)   react and quickly and harshly insult someone

LOUR (lour)

(1)   frown; scowl; dark or threatening

MACHINATE (mak'ə nāt')

(1)   cabal; complot; conspire; devise a plan of evil intent; plan; plot; work out a secret plan

(1) The hackers machinated a way to steal credit numbers from the company's website.

(2)   arrange through systematic planning and a united front

MAKE (ONE'S) BONES

(1)   kill a person as a requirement for membership in a criminal gang, especially if it is one's first murder; to become a made man; (hence) to earn a reputation

(1) The police report showed that Ray killed his own brother to make his bones for the Bloods.

MAZE

(1)   confuse; bewilder; daze; stun the senses by a heavy blow or fatigue; stupefy

MERK (also murk, mirk)

(1)   kill (someone); verbally or physically attack someone; defeat; overcome someone or something; do well

(2)   depart; travel (a place)

MULCT

(1)   take money from someone by a fine or tax, or by dubious means

(2)   deprive by deceit

(1), (2) Partly due to the FDC's secret beginnings and the unpublished minutes of all their meetings, many believe the Fed tends to mulct the public.

NETTLE

(1) annoy; exasperate; grate; irritate by stinging; provoke; vex

(1) Erik's intent was to <u>nettle</u> Bill with constant galimatias chatter.

Antithesis: "Out of this <u>nettle</u>—danger—we pluck this flower—safety."
—William Shakespeare, English dramatist, playwright, and poet (1564–1616)

Parallelism: "Weeds and <u>nettles</u>, briars and thorns, have thriven under your
shadow, dissettlement and division, discontentment and dissatisfaction,
together with real dangers to the whole." —Oliver Cromwell, English military
and political leader and later Lord Protector of the Commonwealth of England
(1599–1658)

Simile: "Tender-handed stroke a <u>nettle</u>,/And it stings you for your pains;/Grasp
it like a man of mettle,/And it soft as silk remains." —Aaron Hill, *A. Hill
Works IV* 120, 1753

Vivid Imagery: "Better to be a <u>nettle</u> in the side of your friend than his echo."
—Ralph Waldo Emerson, American poet, lecturer, and essayist (1803–1882)

OBFUSCATE

(1) baffle; bewilder; complicate; conceal; confuse; disguise; make dim, dark,
or indistinct; mystify; obscure

*(1) It is better to face the consequences of telling the truth than to try to
<u>obfuscate</u>.*

Antithesis: "It's <u>obfuscation</u>. There is no attempt to be clear and concise and
to describe the product for what it is." —Don Catlin, American scientist
(1938–)

OBJURGATE (äb'jər gāt')

(1) blame; chide vehemently; denounce; disapprove; express harshness to a
certain type of behavior; rebuke; revile; upbraid harshly; be vitriolic

(1) Everyone is looking for someone to <u>objurgate</u> for the high gas prices.

OBNUBILATE (äb nōō'b ə lāt')

(1) becloud; darken; make obscure or vague; spurious

OBTRUDE

(1) become obtrusive; impose or force on someone; precocity; terse; turgid;
truculent; surly; interfere, meddle, pry, interrupt, interpose, horn in, intercede; extend, thrust, stick out, push out

(1)   The author's style eventually <u>obtrudes</u> his world view on readers.

(2)   extrude; force one's self or one's ideas on others; thrust out

OCCLUDE

(1)   block or obstruct something, such as a passageway; close or shut; conceal, hide, or obscure something; recalcitrant

PALTER

(1)   act in a trifling or capricious way; be captious; be deliberately ambiguous or unclear in order to mislead; be feckless; flummery; talk insincerely, evasively, or equivocally; indolent; picayune; prevaricate

(2)   deal with facts, decisions, and details in a light or careless way; trifle

PECULATE

(1)   embezzle; defalcate; defraud; steal; misappropriate funds; perfidious

PETTIFOG

(1)   argue over the details; act like a foofaraw; engage in legal trickery; puerile; quibble

RANKLE

(1)   aggravate; annoy; bother; cause bitter and lasting annoyance or resentment; be churlish; exasperate; gall; have long-lasting anger; inflame; infuriate; irk; irritate; needle; rile; rub the wrong way; be snarky

(1)   "Claims that religion can affect health and weight <u>rankle</u> those who see spinning the $40 billion diet industry to a faith-based audience as just a way to use God as a gimmick." —Rona Cherry, "Can You Pray Your Pounds Away?" Vegetarian Times, issue 339, March 2006, p. 80

Antithesis: "If you argue and <u>rankle</u> and contradict, you may achieve a temporary victory—sometimes; but it will be an empty victory because you will never get your opponent's goodwill." —Benjamin Franklin, American statesman, scientist, philosopher, printer, writer, and inventor (1706–1790)

RARK UP

(1)   engage in caterwauling; disturb, annoy, or provoke (someone), especially verbally; chastise or harangue; stimulate, motivate, or excite someone

REASON

(1)   decide by logical thought; present sound arguments; think logically

Antithesis: "Time heals what <u>reason</u> cannot." —Seneca, Roman philosopher, mid–1st century A.D.

Metaphor: "When valor preys on <u>reason</u>, it eats the sword it fights with." — William Shakespeare, English dramatist, playwright, and poet (1564–1616)

Repetition: "It was not <u>reason</u> that besieged Troy; it was not reason that sent forth the Saracen from the desert to conquer the world; that inspired the crusades; that instituted the monastic orders; it was not <u>reason</u> that produced the Jesuits; above all, it was not <u>reason</u> that created the French Revolution. Man is only great when he acts from the passions; never irresistible but when he appeals to the imagination." —Benjamin Disraeli, British prime minister and novelist (1804–1881)

Simile: "<u>Reason</u> is the slow and torturous method by which those who do not know the truth discover." —Blaise Pascal, French mathematician, philosopher, and physicist (1623–1662)

REEF

(1)   use (excessive) force, especially when hitting, pulling, or twisting (on something)

REPROVE

(1)   Admonish; accuse; censure; chide; correct; criticize others; disapprove; haul over the coals; rebuke; reprimand; scold; take to task; tell off

   (1)   "Think not those faithful who praise all thy words and actions; but those who kindly <u>reprove</u> thy faults." —Socrates

ROISTER

(1)   act boisterously; celebrate rowdily; revel noisily

   (1)   "After all this fun, you wish a vacation? Oh, very well, Mathias. I know you are difficult. One week. Go to Elizabethan London. Take in a few plays, drink some sack, <u>roister</u>. That was a good time for <u>roistering</u>. But remember, when you return, you have your work cut out for you." — Alexander Jablokov, The Breath of Suspension

(2)   brag loudly

STONEWALL

(1)   stall, delay, officiate, and refuse to answer questions or cooperate

(1) "Mr. Holder's department stonewalled to block congressional attempts to find out what really happened." —Wall Street Journal, Opinion, 21 June 2012

STULTIFY

(1)   deprive of strength or efficiency

(1) "The perceived threat by most Arabs following the creation of the state of Israel in 1948 contributed to the rise of the military in key Arab countries while creating an atmosphere of belligerency throughout the Arab world. Coupled with the impassioned demands for dismantling Israel, expectations of imminent material prosperity as a consequence of the drive toward modernity managed to stultify democratic appeals." —Halal Khashan, *"The Limits of Arab Democracy,"* World Affairs *153, issue 4, Spring 1991, p. 127*

(2)   be a bumpkin or a couillon; be ineffective; make one's mind dull; nebbish; nescient; stupid; torpid; be of unsound mind; vacuous

SURFEIT

(1)   anything in excess, especially food or drink; flood; glut; surplus; oversupply

TERGIVERSATE *(tŭr'jiv ər sāt')*

(1)   turn one's back on one's cause; make evasive or conflicting statements; equivocate over one's calling; apostatize

TITTLE-TATTLE

(1)   gossipmonger; rumormonger; scandalmonger; tattle

TRADUCE

(1)   attack; accuse falsely of base action; cause humiliation by telling malicious lies about someone; malign; slander; speak unfavorably maliciously about; vilify

(1) "The most powerful, durable, and dangerous special interest—the one that can directly traduce the Constitution—is the political class." —George Will, *"The Court vs. the Reformers; The First Amendment vs. an Arizona Law,"* Newsweek *156, issue 24, 30 December 2010*

TRUCKLE

(1)   be a coxcomb; submit eagerly and subserviently to commands

(2)   be servile; be submissive; cringe; be a toady

> *(1), (2)   "'That's all the more true because at least some of the leaders who avoided service sometimes seem less skeptical about the military than guilt-ridden about their own past. Thirty years later, now elected to positions of prominence, those who evaded service now truckle and fawn to demonstrate the depth of their regard for men in uniform,' writes Andrew J. Bacevich, a professor at Johns Hopkins's School of Advanced International Studies."* —Amy Waldman, "GIs: Not Your Average Joes," Washington Monthly 28, *issue 11, November 1966, p. 26*

UPBRAID

(1)   berate; censure; chasten; chide; criticize; find fault with someone or something; reprimand; scold

> *(1) Supreme Court justices were upbraided by the president during the State of the Union address.*

VEX

(1)   annoy; distress; irritate; plague; provoke; torment; trouble; worry

> *(1)   His family's greed vexed him.*

Antithesis: "Vexed sailors cursed the rain, for which poor shepherds prayed in vain." —Edmund Waller, English poet and politician (1606–1687)

Antithesis: "It vexes me when they would constrain science by the authority of the Scriptures, and yet do not consider themselves bound to answer reason and experiment." —Galileo

Antithesis: "One is always more vexed at losing a game of any sort by a single hole or ace, than if one has never had a chance of winning it." —William Hazlitt, English writer (1778–1830)

Metaphor: "I'll walk where my own nature would be leading: It vexes me to choose another guide." —Emily Bronte, English novelist and poet (1818–1848)

Metaphor: "A very good part of the mischief that vex the world arises from words." —Edmund Burke, British statesman and philosopher (1729–1797)

Repetition: "The greatest crimes are to associate another with God, to vex your father and mother, to murder your own species, to commit suicide, and to swear to lie." —Muhammad, religious leader, prophet of Islam

VILIFY

(1)   use abusive, slanderous language; belittle; criticize; defame; do a hatchet job on; disparage; insult; libel; malign; pilloried; pull to pieces; rail; revile; run down; sensor; slander; speak ill of

   (1) Political speeches have become an excuse to <u>vilify</u> one's opponent.

Parallelism: "They have <u>vilified</u> me, they have crucified me; yes, they have even criticized me." Richard J. Daley, former Chicago mayor (1902–1976)

Repetition: "<u>Vilify</u>, <u>vilify</u>, <u>vilify</u>, some of it will always stick." —Pierre Beaumarchais, French playwright, watchmaker, inventor, musician, diplomat, fugitive, and spy (1732–1799)

Simile: "To <u>vilify</u> a great man is the readiest way in which a little man can himself attain greatness." —Edgar Allan Poe

VILIPEND

(1)   contemn; deprecate; disparage; speak ill of; view or treat with contempt; despise; vilify

   (1) He is one of those elitists who regularly <u>vilipends</u> popular culture.

VITIATE

(1)   cause to fail, either wholly or in part; make void; destroy as the validity or binding force of an instrument or transaction; annul; make vicious, faulty, or imperfect; render defective; injure the substance or qualities of; impair; contaminate; make void; destroy, as the validity or binding force of an instrument or transaction; spoil.

   (1) "Saint Augustine wished to exclude any necessarily illusory utopianism from human hope here below. Even with his full complement of secular pessimism, Augustine was not advocating cruel and arbitrary rule, for he knew well how wicked motives could <u>vitiate</u> an otherwise well-governed state." —Fredrick Russell, "Only Something Good Can Be Evil: The Secular Genesis of Augustine's Secular Ambivalence," Theological Studies *51, issue 4, December 1990, p. 698*

(2)   impure; make unclean; pollute

(3)   make corrupt; faulty; imperfect; invalidate; spoil

VITUPERATE

(1) berate; scold; speak harshly or viciously about something

> *(1) "The Yugoslavian-born poet Charles Simic has said, 'There are moments in life when true invective is called for, when it becomes an absolute necessity, out of a deep sense of justice, to denounce, mock, <u>vituperate</u>, lash out, in the strongest possible language.' We have come to such a moment. Leaving aside invective, <u>vituperation</u>, and mockery, I believe that we need space for peaceful yet passionate outrage."*
> —Deborah Tannen, "We Need Higher Quality Outrage," Christian Science Monitor, 2004

VOCIFERATE

(1) clamor; bawl; speak or say loudly or nosily; shout

YAMMER

(1) complain in a whiney, wimpy fashion

(2) shout, yell, clamor

(3) talk loudly and continually

YAWP

(1) talk noisily and foolishly or complain

POSITIVE HUMAN BEHAVIOR

ACHIEVE

(1) accomplish; attain; bring to a successful end; complete; conclude; do; finish; get; reach; perform; pull off; realize

(2) succeed in doing something

> *(1), (2) "Some men are born mediocre, some men <u>achieve</u> mediocrity, and some men have mediocrity thrust upon them. —Joseph Heller, American satirical novelist, short story writer, and playwright (1923–1999)*

> *(1), (2) "That some <u>achieve</u> great success, is proof to all that others can <u>achieve</u> it as well." —President Abraham Lincoln*

Antithesis: "To <u>achieve</u> great things, two things are needed: a plan, and not quite enough time." —Leonard Bernstein, American conductor, composer, and pianist (1918–1990)

Antithesis: "A creative man is motivated by the desire to <u>achieve</u>, not by the desire to beat others." —Ayn Rand

Antithesis: "It is easy to hate and it is difficult to love. This is how the whole scheme of things works. All good things are difficult to <u>achieve</u>; and bad things are very easy to get." —Confucius

Parallelism: "The more you seek security, the less of it you have. But the more you seek opportunity, the more likely it is that you will <u>achieve</u> the security that you desire." —Bryan Tracy, self-help author, motivational speaker, entrepreneur, and business coach (1944–)

Parallelism: "If you can dream it, then you can <u>achieve</u> it. You will get all you want in life if you help enough other people get what they want." —Zig Zigler, motivational speaker (1926–2012)

ACQUIESCE

(1) accept; agree; assent; consent; comply with passively; concur; concede; consent; give in; go along with; submit; yield

(1) It was an important sign of personal growth for Joe to <u>acquiesce</u> to a plan he originally did not like.

<u>Collocates to: agree, accept, compelled, expect, forced, should, would</u>

ADAPT

(1) acclimate; accommodate; adjust; change; conform; fashion; fit; get used to; make suitable; reconcile; square; suit; tailor

(1) The ability to <u>adapt</u> to change is an important characteristic that employers look for in applicants.

(2) make fit, often by modification

(3) cause something to change for the better

Alliteration: With today's rapid changes in technology, we can <u>a</u>dapt, <u>a</u>cclimate, <u>a</u>djust, <u>a</u>ccommodate, or <u>a</u>ccept an <u>a</u>lteration in the quality of our <u>a</u>nticipated lifestyle.

Metaphor: "The key to success is often the ability to <u>adapt</u>." —Unknown

Metaphor: "<u>Adapt</u> yourself to the things among which your lot has been cast and love sincerely the fellow creatures with whom destiny has ordained that you shall live." —Marcus Aurelius, Roman emperor (A.D. 121–180)

Metaphor: "<u>Adapt</u> or perish, now as ever, is nature's inexorable imperative." —H.G. Wells, English author (1866–1946)

Parallelism: "The reasonable man adapts himself to the world; the unreasonable one persists in trying to adapt the world to himself. Therefore, all progress depends on the unreasonable man." —George Bernard Shaw, Irish literary critic, playwright, essayist, and winner of the 1925 Nobel Prize for Literature (1856–1950)

Simile: "The wise adapt themselves to circumstances, as water molds itself to the pitcher." —Chinese proverb

Vivid imagery: "We talk of our mastery of nature, which sounds very grand; but the fact is, we respectfully adapt ourselves, first, to her ways." —Clarence Day, American humorist, essayist, biographer, and writer (1874–1935)

ASSIGN

(1) allot; appoint; apportion; ascribe; attribute; delegate; designate; impute; portion; put; repute; set apart; specify

Alliteration: If you are to succeed, you must do what you are allotted, take up all you are assigned and apportioned, and set out to achieve.

Antithesis: "We trifle when we assign limits to our desires, since nature hath set none." —Christian Nestell Bovee, American author (1820–1880)

Metaphor: "You cannot paint the *Mona Lisa* by assigning one dab of paint each to a thousand painters." —William F. Buckley, Jr., American writer (1925–2008)

Vivid imagery: "It is the eye of ignorance that assigns a fixed and unchangeable color to every object; beware of this stumbling block." —Paul Gauguin, French post-Impressionist artist (1848–1903)

AUSPICATE

(1) augur; begin a ceremony intended to bring on good luck

AVER

(1) affirm; assert the truthfulness of something; avow; claim; declare; maintain; profess; state; swear

(1) Some philosophers aver that both moral blame and legal responsibility should be based on prior behavior.

(1) "The anti-reformer is Chuck Schumer, the Senator from Wall Street, New York, who averred at the National Press Club last week that his party will have nothing to do with tax reform of the kind that Ronald Reagan negotiated with Democrats in 1989, or that the Simpson–Bowles

deficit commission proposed in 2010, or that the Gang of Six Senators have been working on. It's Chuck's way or no way." —Wall Street Journal, *Opinion, 15 October 2012*

Metaphor: "I know the thing that's most uncommon
(Envy be silent and attend!);
I know a reasonable woman,
Handsome and witty, yet a friend.

Not warped by passion, awed by rumor,
Not grave through pride, or gay through folly;
An equal mixture of good humor
And sensible soft melancholy.

'Has she no faults, then (Envy says), sir?'
Yes, she has one, I must <u>aver</u>:
When all the world conspires to praise her,
The woman's deaf, and does not hear."

—Alexander Pope, British poet (1688–1744); "On a Certain Lady at Court"

AVOW

(1)   acknowledge; affirm; admit publicly; assert; aver; claim; declare boldly; maintain; state

   (1) "I <u>avow</u> myself the partisan of truth alone." —William Harvey, English physician (1578–1657)

Alliteration: If you set out to <u>avow</u> something and then <u>a</u>cknowledge you are pledging your name, <u>a</u>ffirming your consciousness, and <u>a</u>dmitting publicly, you are <u>a</u>sserting your honor.

Antithesis: "Cautious, careful people always casting about to preserve their reputation or social standards never can bring about reform. Those who are really in earnest are willing to be anything or nothing in the world's estimation, and publicly and privately, in season and out, <u>avow</u> their sympathies with despised ideas and their advocates, and bear the consequences." —Susan B. Anthony

CHOPE (slang)

(1)   to reserve something such as a seat, place, or book

   (1) It's free seating at the concert; we need to get there early to <u>chope</u> seats for our group.

CLARIFY (A POINT)

(1)   clear up; elucidate; illuminate; make something clearer by explaining it in greater detail; shed light on; simplify; spell out

Antithesis: "Like other revolutionaries, I can thank God for the reactionaries. They clarify the issue." —Robin G. Collingwood, English philosopher (1889–1943)

Parallelism: "By speaking, by thinking, we undertake to clarify things, and that forces us to exacerbate them, dislocate them, schematize them. Every concept is in itself an exaggeration." —Jose Ortega y Gasset, Spanish philosopher and humanist (1883–1955)

Repetition: "Matisse makes a drawing, then he makes a copy of it. He recopies it five times, ten times, always clarifying the line. He's convinced that the last, the most stripped down, is the best, the purest, the definitive one; and in fact, most of the time, it was the first. In drawing, nothing is better than the first attempt." —Pablo Picasso, Spanish artist and painter (1881–1973)

Repetition: "Generally speaking, men are influenced by books which clarify their own thought, which express their own notions well, or which suggest to them ideas which their minds are already predisposed to accept." —Carl Becker, American historian (1873–1945)

Simile: "I use my hands *like* a sculptor, to mold and shape the sound I want, to clarify." —Leonard Slatkin, American conductor and composer (1944–)

COMFORT

(1)   give moral support; help with emotional support; lessen pain or discomfort

   (1) She is always the first to offer comfort to others in need.

Metaphor: "It may serve as a comfort to us, in all our calamities and afflictions, that he that loses anything and gets wisdom by it is a gainer by the loss." —Sir Roger L. Estrange, English pamphleteer and author (1616–1704)

Antithesis: "Comfort and prosperity have never enriched the world as much as adversity has." —Billy Graham, American Christian evangelist (1918–)

CONFIDE

(1)   confer a trust upon; reveal in private: tell in confidence

   (1) Don't confide in someone to whom you would not loan money.

Antithesis: "We confide in our strength, without boasting of it; we respect that of others, without fearing it." —President Thomas Jefferson and author of the Declaration of Independence (1743–1826)

Metaphor: "None are deceived but they that confide." —Benjamin Franklin, American statesman, scientist, philosopher, printer, writer, and inventor (1706–1790)

Vivid imagery: "We rarely confide in those who are better than we are." —Albert Camus, French novelist, essayist, playwright, and winner of the 1957 Nobel Prize for Literature (1913–1960)

CORUSCATE

(1) brilliant in style; flashy; showy; sparkle

(1) "Claude Monet's 1873 Boulevard des Capucines records an outsider's distant glimpse of numerous pedestrians who register not as thoughtful individuals, but as an anonymous crowd of figures whose external surfaces coruscate and dissolve in the ambient light particles that form their atmosphere." —Nancy Forgione, "Everyday Life in Motion: The Art of Walking in Late-Nineteenth-Century Paris," Art Bulletin 87, issue 4, December 2005, p. 664–687

COUNSEL

(1) advise; deliberate; inform

(1) "Counsel and conservation are a secondary education, which improve all the virtue, and correct all the vice of the first, and nature itself." —Edward Hyde Clarendon, British statesman and historian (1609–1674)

DISABUSE

(1) correct; enlighten; free one from an incorrect assumption or belief

(1) His mentor was able to disabuse Trevor of the notion that there was something wrong with networking one's way to success.

(2) admonish strongly; encourage earnestly by advice or warning; insist; press; push; urge

Metaphor: "Chaos of thought and passion, all confused; Still by himself abused or disabused; Created half to rise, and half to fall; Great lord of all things, yet a prey to all; Sole judge of truth, in endless error hurled, —The glory, jest, and riddle of the world." —Alexander Pope, English poet (1688–1744)

EXHORT

(1)   barrack, cheer, inspire; press; urge

Simile: "I exhort you also to take part in the great combat, which is the combat of life, and greater than every other earthly combat." —Plato

GIBE (jīb) (also see Human Behavior and Experience, Negative Behavior)

(1)   heckle; jeer; laugh at with contempt and derision; mock; scoff; taunt

   (1) A well-placed zinger in a political contest is quite natural, but to gibe with personal attacks is over-the-top behavior.

(2)   be compatible, similar, or consistent

MELIORATE (mēl'yə rāt')

(1)   better; improve; grow; make something better or stronger

   (1) You can meliorate a potential tax burden on your children at your death by insurance gifts while you're alive.

MOLLIFY

(1)   appease; assuage; calm; conciliate; pacify; placate; season; soften; soothe; temper

   (1) With the approach of the 2012 election, the President has appeared too eager to mollify his base and abandon business interests.

MOLLYCODDLE

(1)   baby; cater to; cosset; fuss over; humor; indulge; mamma's boy; overprotect; pamper; spoil

   (1) It doesn't necessarily help nor harm a person to mollycoddle him or her; the overdoing is the problem.

PERSEVERE

(1)   be steadfast in purpose; continue in some effort or course of action in spite of difficulty or opposition; persist

   (1) "Victory belongs to the most persevering." —Napoleon Bonaparte

PROPITIATE (prō pish' ē āt')

(1)   appease; atone; conciliate; favor; gain approval; like best; placate; win over

Metaphor: "The cloud was so dark that it needed all the bright lights that could be turned upon it. But for four years there was a contagion of nobility in the land, and the best blood North and South poured itself out a libation to propitiate the deities of Truth and Justice. The great sin of slavery was washed out, but at what a cost!" —M. E. W. Sherwood, American author (1826–1903); *An Epistle to Posterity*

RATIOCINATE (rash'ē äs'ə nāt')

(1) deductive argument; sagacious; work toward a solution through logical thinking and reason

(1) When you come down to it, there is too much ratiocination in the debates and too few solutions based on practical common sense.

RECRUDESCE

(1) back up, bounce back; break out; become active again after a period of latency; circle back; refresh; rebound; recoil; recover vitality; repair: return; revive; vigor

Alliteration: My recrudesce began with a rebound of recovered vitality concurrent with the repairs to my ranch house.

SAUNTER (sôn't r)

(1) amble; move along with no apparent aim or direction; stroll; walk at a leisurely pace; stroll in a casual manner

SEAGULL

(1) hang back and await an opportunity to benefit from desirable circumstances found or created by other people

(1) David's plan was to seagull out of sight while the party faithful took the heat for the fundraising scandal.

SET-JET

(1) visit as a tourist in a place used as a filming location in a movie or television show; participate in movie tourism or film tourism

SUCCOR

(1) assist; encourage; give assistance in time of need

(1) "The new Russian government promised to <u>succor</u> ailing mining, industrial and agricultural giants with trillions of rubles in new credits— and in virtually every sector, sensing the change in political winds, workers staged or threatened strikes to demand more." —Margaret Shapiro and Fred Hiatt, "Russia Tries Reform—Is it Working?" Washington Post, *1994*

TITIVATE

(1) adorn; dress up; spruce up; put finishing touch on

TRIP ALONG

(1) move with a careless or leisurely gait; leisurely move about; saunter; to move along happily

(1) The kids <u>tripped along</u> on their way to school.

VOUCHSAFE

(1) give or grant in a gracious or condescending manner

WHEEDLE

(1) coax; persuade or obtain by coaxing

(1) "Harpring almost wound up at Duke or Northwestern on a football scholarship because his efforts to <u>wheedle</u> a basketball grant-in-aid out of Tech coach Bobby Cremins were going nowhere." —Alexander Wolff, "Thrills and Spills," Sports Illustrated *84, issue 12, March 1996, p. 36*

ZONE IN

(1) focus on something intently

NATURE AND CLIMATE

ESTIVATE (es't' vāt')

(1) spend the summer in a dormant state; spend a lazy summer relaxing and doing no work

FECUNDATE

(1) make fertile or productive

PIXIE

(1) practice sabotage as an expression of environmental politics

8

Matter and Energy: Physical Properties

ABSORB

(1) cause to become one

(1) Oxygen is <u>absorbed</u> into the bloodstream by the lungs.

(2) devote oneself fully to something

(3) take up mentally

ATTENUATE

(1) become weaker in strength, value, or magnitude; lessen; make less consistent; thin or slender

AUTHENTICATE

(1) confirm; endorse; establish as genuine, make authoritative or valid; serve to prove; substantiate; validate

(1) The bank's servers must be able to <u>authenticate</u> remote customers who request services or applications.

<u>Collocates to: claim, document, further, identity, service, text, user, validate, verify</u>

CARBON SEQUESTER

(1) acquire, absorb, and store carbon dioxide from the atmosphere by man-made means

(1) Examples of carbon sequestering include major climatic fluctuations, such as the Azolla event, which created the current Arctic climate. Such processes created fossil fuels, as well as clathrate or limestone. By manipulating such processes, geoengineers plan to <u>carbon sequester</u> carbon dioxide.

CLEAR-CUT

(1) remove, in a single cutting, all the trees within a designated area

CONSERVE

(1) keep safe and protect from harm, decay, loss, or destruction

(2) keep constant through chemical or physical reactions or evolutionary process

CULL

(1) remove something that nature or humans have rejected; pick out for rejection any item from a production because it does not meet certain specifications

(2) look for and gather

(3) cull out—to select the most desirable from a group or list

9

Religion: Ethics and Morality

ABSOLUTIZE (ab-sə-'lŭ-'tīz)

(1)   change to a moral principle; convert into an absolute; make absolute

(1) According to Merriam-Webster, the first known use of the word absolutize was in 1919.

AFFECT

(1)   connect closely, sometimes inappropriately or in a fabricated, deceptive, or insincere manner; have an emotional or cognitive impact upon; make believe with a possible intent to deceive; unreal approach to something

(1) "Words not only affect us temporarily; they change us, they socialize or unsocialize us." —David Riesman, American sociologist, attorney, and educator (1909–2002)

Antithesis: "People will always talk about you, especially when they envy you and the life you live. Let them ... you affected their lives, they didn't affect yours." —Unknown

Metaphor: "To affect the quality of the day, that is the highest of the arts." —Henry David Thoreau, American essayist, poet, and philosopher (1817–1862)

Parallelism: "Other people's acts will affect just them. It is only your own deeds that will affect you." —Sri Sathya Sai Baba, Indian spiritual leader (1926–)

Repetition: "Little things affect little minds." —Benjamin Disraeli, British prime minister and novelist (1804–1881)

Repetition: "The difficulty of literature is not to write, but to write what you mean; not to affect your reader, but to affect him precisely as you wish." —Robert Louis Stevenson, Scottish essayist, poet, and author (1850–1894)

ANOINT

(1) rub oil or ointment

(2) put oil on in a ceremony of consecration

ARROGATE

(1) assume; ascribe; claim as own; take power that is not yours

(1) "We believe that the federal judiciary's attempt to <u>arrogate</u> to itself sole responsibility for resolving the profound moral and legal issues engaged by the abortion debate is undemocratic." —George Wiegel and William Kristol, "Life and the Party," National Review, *15 July 1994*

ASSUAGE (əs'wāj')

(1) appease; erase doubts and fears; mollify; pacify; satisfy; soothe

(1) I worked to <u>assuage</u> my own guilt over the incident.

<u>Collocates to: anger, anguish, anxiety, concerns, consciences, curiosity, doubt, feelings, fears, guilt, hunger, hurt, loneliness, pride, worries</u>

ASSURE (əs'hoor')

(1) comfort; convince; declare; ensure; give surety; guarantee; insure; pledge; promise; reassure; swear

(2) ensure; confirm; know for sure; nail down; substantiate; verify

Parallelism: "I <u>assure</u> you that a learned fool is more foolish than an ignorant fool." —Moliere, French actor, playwright, and writer (1622–1673)

Parallelism: "We cannot always <u>assure</u> the future of our friends; we have a better chance of assuring our future if we remember who our friends are." —Henry Kissinger, German-born American writer, political scientist, and former Secretary of State (1923–)

ATTITUDINIZE

(1) assume certain affected attitudes; pose for effect; strike an attitude

(1) In the book, Masters of the Universe, *Daniel Stedman Jones, a barrister in London, covers the same ground and has intelligent things to say, but his book's historical virtues are compromised by more adjectival <u>attitudinizing</u> than a chronicler of history should allow himself." —Kenneth Minogue, "The Death and Life of Liberal Economics," book review, "Books,"* Wall Street Journal *27–28 October 2012, p. C5*

COALESCE

(1) amalgamate, blend or come together; conflate; flux; fuse; grow together into one body; mix together; single-mindedness of purpose; unite as to form one

Alliteration: After a time the course of the currents of two conflating rivers caused them to coalesce.

Metaphor: "After a certain high level of technical skill is achieved, science and art tend to coalesce in esthetics, plasticity, and form. The greatest scientists are always artists as well." —Albert Einstein (1879–1955)

Collocates to: begin, around, elements form into, opportunities, single

COMPORT (kom'-port)

(1) act; acquit; agree; bear; behave in a certain way that is proper; carry; conduct

(1) Recent movies seem to give a favorable view of the way the troops comport themselves in combat.

Metaphor: "I believe you have a responsibility to comport yourself in a manner that gives an example to others. As a young man, I prayed for success. Now I pray just to be worthy of it." —Brendan Fraser, Canadian-American film and stage actor (1968–)

Vivid imagery: "In the wars of the European powers in matters relating to themselves we have never taken any part, nor does it comport with our policy so to do." —President James Monroe

"Individuality is the aim of political liberty. By leaving the citizen as much freedom of action and of being as comports with order and the rights of others, the institutions render him truly a freeman. He is left to pursue his means of happiness in his own manner." —James Fenimore Cooper, American writer of the early 19th century (1789–1851)

Collocates to: does, dress, dogma, himself, facts, governance, how, ideas, laws, manner, themselves, yourself, with, values

CONDOLE

(1) comfort another; express sympathy

(1) In the biblical parable of Job, his friends defamed rather than condoled him.

CONFIDE

(1)   confer a trust; reveal in private

(1) "We rarely confide in those who are better than we are." —Albert Camus, French novelist, essayist, playwright, and winner of 1957 Nobel Prize for Literature (1913–1960)

Collocates to: anyone, courage, fears, feeling, friends, innermost, likely, someone, secrets, trust, whom

CONFUTE

(1)   disapprove; prove to be false or wrong; refute; reject

(1) "Ignorance of the law excuses no man; not that all men know the law, but because [']tis an excuse every man will plead, and no man can tell how to confute him." —John Seldon, English jurist and scholar (1584–1654)

(2)   make useless

Alliteration: "The arguments for purity of life fail of their due influence, not because they have been considered and confuted, but because they have been passed over without consideration." —Samuel Johnson, English poet, critic, and writer (1709–1784)

Antithesis: "To command the professors of astronomy to confute their own observations is to enjoin impossibility, for it is to command them not to see what they do see, and not to understand what they do understand, and to find what they do not discover." —Galileo Galilei, Italian natural philosopher, astronomer, and mathematician (1564–1642)

Parallelism: "Read not to contradict and confute; nor to believe and take for granted; nor to find talk and discourse; but to weigh and consider." —Francis Bacon, British philosopher (1561–1626), in "Of Studies"

Vivid imagery: "Do not attempt to confute a lion after he's dead." —the Talmud

CONNIVE

(1)   avoid noticing something; cooperate secretly or have a secret understanding; encounter or assent to illegal or criminal act; form intrigue in an underhanded manner; pretend ignorance or fail to take action; look the other way; plot a secret plan; scheme

Alliteration: "It is a matter of common knowledge that the government of South Carolina is under domination of a small ring of cunning, conniving men." —Sen. Strom Thurmond

Antithesis: "God cannot alter the past; that is why he is obliged to connive at the existence of historians." —Samuel Butler, English novelist, essayist, and critic (1835–1902)

Antithesis: "If they had connived a scheme, and Christ had not been raised from the dead, where would have been the hardest place on the face of the earth to convince anyone? In Jerusalem." —Josh McDowell, Christian apologist, evangelist, and writer (1939–)

CONSECRATE

(1)   devote; make or declare sacred; sanctify; set apart as holy

(1) To consecrate his life to something greater than himself, he joined a silent order of monks.

CONTRADISTINGUISH

(1)   contrast; distinguish by contrasting qualities; reveal differences; show disparity

(1) His work is in sharp contradistinction to the view of competition as a state of equilibrium induced by a particular market structure.

Antithesis: "These are our complex ideas of soul and body, as contradistinguished." —John Locke, English philosopher and physician (1632–1704)

COZEN

(1)   beguile; cheat; defraud; delude; lead on; nefarious; trick

(1) Politicians will frequently cozen if they think it will further their political ends.

CUMBER

(1)   charge; constrain; burden; hinder by obstruction or interference; place heavy burden on; restrain

DEROGATE

(1) belittle; detract; disparage; take away; impair

*(1) "George has suggested that nothing would so seriously derogate American representative government as the allocation of American forces to non-American control for missions not chosen by persons directly accountable to American voters." —*Bruce Weinrod, *"The U.S. Role in Peacekeeping-Related Activities,"* World Affairs *155, issue 4, Spring 1993, p. 148*

DESECRATE

(1) blaspheme; damage; defile; despoil; be diabolical; insult; lay waste; outrage; profane; vandalize; violate

(1) "This was a mutual relationship, mutual on all levels, right from the way it started and all the way through. I don't accept that he had to completely desecrate my character." —Monica Lewinsky, American woman with whom United States President Bill Clinton admitted to having had an "improper relationship" (1973–)

Collocates to: body, dead, desire, flag, graves, land, religious, sacred

DISCRIMINATE

(1) identify, notice, or single out the difference between some things

(2) be discerning; biased; differentiate; notice incompatible differences; be partial; prejudice; make unequal; unequal

DISENFRANCHISE

(1) deny someone a right or privilege; make someone feel rejected or separate

ESPOUSE *(also see Education and Communications)*

(1) adopt; advocate; back; champion; promote; support; take up

(1) The governor espoused a program of tax cuts.

(2) take as a wife

EVISCERATE *(ē vis'ər āt')*

(1) deprive of an essential part; take away the force or significance of

(2) cause or experience a protrusion

(3)   disembowel

(1) His extensive knowledge of the topic and his sharp retorts helped eviscerate his debating opponent.

EXECRATE (ek'si krāt')

(1)   hate; use profane language; regard with extreme dislike; swear
(2)   curse or call evil down upon
(3)   speak abusively of; be contemptuous of; denounce scathingly
(4)   abhor; detest; loathe

INDURATE

(1)   feel no compassion; be physically or morally hardened; be callous or unfeeling
(2)   become accustomed
(3)   make or become hard

LUSTRATE (lus'trāt')

(1)   be free from guilt or defilement; purify

MALEDICT (mal'ə dikt')

(1)   curse; bring evil or injury upon

MELIORATE

(1)   improve; make something better

MILITATE

(1)   have a substantial effect on; weigh heavily on

OPINE

(1)   harangue; discourse; go on; hold, express, or give an opinion; lecture; orate; preach; rant; stress something; speak out; suppose; think

(1) You can opine about what employers should care about, but their primary concern is whether you will fit in.

SANCTIFY

(1)   consecrate; make holy; make legitimate or binding by religious sanction; give the appearance of being right or good

(2)   make morally right or binding

TEMPOR

(1)   restrain; make more temperate, acceptable, or suitable

(2)   bring to a desired consistency, texture, or hardness by a process of gradual heating and cooling

(1), (2) "We dare not forget today that we are the heirs of that first revolution. Let the word go forth from this time and place, to friend and foe alike, that the torch has been passed to a new generation of Americans— born in this century, tempered by war, disciplined by a hard and bitter peace, proud of our ancient heritage, and unwilling to witness or permit the slow undoing of those human rights to which this nation has always been committed, and to which we are committed today at home and around the world." —John F. Kennedy, presidential inaugural address, 19 January 1961

(3)   harden by reheating and cooling in oil

VENERATE

(1)   honor as sacred or noble; respect deeply; revere

(2)   look upon with feelings of deep respect; regard as venerable

(1) "One reason why George Washington is held in such veneration: He never blamed his problems on the former administration." —Unknown

Collocates to: academic, blessed, Christians, constitution, cross, culture, faith, family, image, Mary

10

Society and Social Organizations: Culture, Business Concepts and Economics, Education, Law, Politics and Government, Social Groups, and Organizations

General Personal Behavior, Character, Characteristics, Traits, and Skills

ACCULTURATE

(1) cause (a society, for example) to change by the process of acculturation; change behavior to suit a new culture

(1) In most cases, by the third generation, most immigrant ethnic groups have begun to assimilate and acculturate, *thus becoming more like members of the native population.*

ADDUCE (also see Law)

(1) allege; bring forward; cite as evidence; lead to; present; put forward

(1) "Whoever in discussion adduces *authority uses not intellect, but memory." —Leonardo da Vinci*

ADJUDICATE (əjoo-'di kāt')

(1)   act as judge; listen; mediate; preside over argument; settle

     (1) Susan tried her best to adjudicate the dispute as the sales team argued back and forth over the commission plan.

ADUMBRATE

(1)   foreshadow; give a general description of something but not the details; prefigure; obscure; overshadow; predict; presage; summarize

ADVISE

(1)   counsel; direct; give advice; give opinion; recommend; warn

(2)   inform; let know; make aware; notify; tell someone what has happened

AGGLOMERATE

(1)   accumulate; cluster; gather together; jumbled collection

AGGRANDIZE

(1)   exalt; increase; make greater; make larger; puffery

     (1) He tried to aggrandize his own role in the jury deliberations.

AMELIORATE (əmēl'yə rāt')

(1)   correct a mistake; improve; make better; tolerate

     (1) Phillip ameliorated the issues in the business plan prior to the meeting with the investors.

(2)   correct a deficiency or defect; make right a wrong; take action that makes up for one's negative or improper actions

ANALOGIZE

(1)   break down; dissect; liken; resolve

ANIMATE (an'i māt')

(1)   give life to; give sprit and support to; quicken

(2)   make or design in such a way as to create apparently spontaneous lifelike movement

ANNUNCIATE

(1)   announce; bring to public notice; proclaim; make known

ARBITRATE (är'bə trāt')

(1)   adjudicate; decide; intercede; judge; mediate; negotiate; pass judgment; referee; settle; sort out

ASSERT

(1)   affirm; allege; contend; aver; avow; claim; declare; emphasize; protest; state strongly; stress

(2)   champion; defend; establish; insist upon; maintain; make a claim for; stand up for; support; uphold

(1), (2) "First of all, let me assert my firm belief that the only thing we have to fear is fear itself—nameless, unreasoning, unjustified terror which paralyzes needed efforts to convert retreat into advance."
—President Franklin D. Roosevelt, 4 March 1933

ASSEVERATE

(1)   assert; aver; avouch; avow; declare earnestly or solemnly; hold; maintain

(1) "I hereby do asseverate my solemn belief that globalization, taken as a whole, is a positive economic force and well worth defending."
—Timothy Taylor, "The Truth About Globalization," Public Interest, issue 147, Spring 2002, p. 24

ASSUAGE

(1)   appease; erase doubts and fears; mollify; pacify; satisfy; soothe

ATTENUATE

(1)   dilute; enervate; make thin or slender; weaken or reduce in force, intensity, effect, quality, or value

AUGUR

(1)   auspicate; betoken; bode; divine; forebode; foreshadow; foretell; portend; predict

(1) "The single best augury is to fight for one's country." —Homer

BUMP THE SHARK

(1) push back against an aggressive person; stand up against an intrusive, aggressive, or assertive verbal assault

(2) fight back against a bully

(1), (2) The last thing the thug expected from a gray-haired woman with a walker was someone who was ready to <u>bump the shark</u>.

COMMISERATE

(1) feel empathy; express sympathy; feel compassion or pity; sympathize

CONGREGATE

(1) assemble; come together; felicitate; gather

CONSIGN

(1) agree; dispatch; entrust; give over or commit to others; pack off; relegate; submit

(2) deliver; send; transfer

(1) "The Presidency of Jimmy Carter in the United States and the government of James Callaghan in 1970s Britain, Mr. Stedman Jones writes, were already liberating economies from controls under which they had suffered (for so long). Such follies as wage-price controls and fixed exchange rates were already being <u>consigned</u> to history."
—Kenneth Minogue, "The Death and Life of Liberal Economics,"
Wall Street Journal, *27–28 October 2012, p. C5*

CONTRADISTINGUISH

(1) contrast; reveal differences; show disparity

CORROBORATE

(1) back; back up with evidence; confirm formally; make certain the validity of; strengthen; support a statement or argument with evidence

COUNTENANCE

(1) approve; encourage; favorably disposed; sanction; support

COUNTERVAIL

(1) avail against; balance; compensate; equalize; make up for

ENOUNCE

(1) speak, pronounce, or utter words in a certain way

ENSCONCE

(1) place or settle comfortably, snuggly, or securely

(2) conceal; establish; entrench; install; hide; shelter

ENTREAT

(1) beg; beseech; implore; intercede; negotiate; plead; pray; request earnestly or emotionally

ESCHEW (es c/hoo')

(1) abstain; avoid; disdain; give up; have nothing to do with; keep away from; shun; steer clear of; turn your back on

(1) In today's reform-minded political climate, elected officials are eschewing lobbyists with poor reputations.

EVOLVE

(1) develop by gradual changes; derive; elaborate

(2) set free; give off

(3) produce or change by evolution

GALUMP

(1) move or run slowly or clumsily

(2) transport someone or something

GAMBOL

(1) caper; cavort; dance; frisk; prance; rollick; romp; run; skip; jump in a playful or joyous fashion

(1) During the run-up to the financial bubble of 2008–2010, many financial planners allowed their less informed clients to gambol forth into questionable direct investments like junk bonds and real estate developments.

GLAVER *(glăv-er)*

(1)   complement excessively; flatter; be obsequious

GLISSADE *(gli sād')*

(1)   glide; move smoothly and effortlessly

GRABBLE

(1)   feel or search with hands; grope

(2)   lie or fall prone; sprawl; scramble about

GUFFAW

(1)   break up laughing; express great amusement or mirth

IMBUE

(1)   indoctrinate; instill

(1)   "Education would be so much more effective if its purpose were to ensure that by the time they leave school, every boy and girl should know how much they don't know, and be <u>imbued</u> with a lifelong desire to know it." —Sir William Haley, British newspaper editor and broadcasting administrator (1901–1987)

(2)   drink; endow; fill; infuse; permeate or take in moisture

IMMURE *(I myo-or')*

(1)   build into a wall; confine; detain; enclose; jail; imprison; incarcerate; intern; seclude; shut away; shut in; put someone in a place with no escape

IMPUGN *(im pyōōn')*

(1)   attack as false or wrong by argument or criticism; challenge something as false or wrong; express doubts about the truth or honesty of someone

(1)   "Although Holden was mistaken about the origin of lunar craters like Copernicus, it would be churlish to <u>impugn</u> him too harshly on this matter, as many other astronomers thought similarly." —Graeme Smith, "Refining Refracted Moonlight," Mercury 33, issue 5, Sept./Oct. 2004, p. 30–38

IMPUTE

(1) accuse; allege; assert; challenge; charge; cite; implicate

(2) accredit; attribute; ascribe a result or quality to anything or anyone; assign; fix

INTERPOSE

(1) aggressive; arbitrate; insert; intercept; interfere; intermediate; meddle; mediate; unsolicited opinion; offer assistance or presence; put between

INTUIT

(1) know something instinctively through direct instinct

METE

(1) allot; set aside or distribute a share; measure

MEW

(1) confine; enclose

NUT UP

(1) become bold, courageous, or forthright; sack up, man up

OBSECRATE

(1) beg; beseech; plead; supplicate

QUAFF

(1) drink with gusto and in large volume; imbibe; swill; guzzle

SATIATE

(1) satisfy an appetite fully; gratify completely; glut with an excess of something; provide with more than enough

(1) "The 'Connection Principle' is the unconscious intention to <u>satiate</u> hunger with food and simply reflects some biological aspect of the brains workings that has the capacity to produce conscious appetite and food seeking behavior in certain situations." —Bruce Bower, "Rethinking the Mind," Science News *142, issue 16, 17 October 1992, p. 264*

<u>Collocates to: appetite, ate, desire, food, hunger, need, wealth</u>

SAUNTER

(1) amble; meander; mosey; promenade; ramble; stroll; walk idly about

(1) "The really efficient laborer will be found not to crowd his day with work, but will saunter to his task surrounded by a wide halo of ease and leisure." —Henry David Thoreau, American essayist, poet, and philosopher (1817–1862)

Metaphor: "Reading without purpose is sauntering, not exercise." —Edward G. Bulwer-Lytton, British politician, poet, critic, and prolific novelist (1803–1873)

SCINTILLATE

(1) flash; sparkle; sizzle

(2) sparkle intellectually; be brilliant and witty

(3) twinkle, as a star

SCREW THE POOCH (slang)

(1) foul up; make a mistake; mess up

SPANG (also Spange)

(1) panhandle; beg for money

SPAVE

(1) spend money under the illusion that one is saving money

SPIT GAME

(1) flirt with, hit on, or try to pick up a woman

SPLAY

(1) move out of position; turn outward

(2) spread open or apart

SQUICK

(1) disturb, unsettle, make uneasy; cause disgust or revulsion; gross someone out; freak someone

(1) Some things are too repulsive to discuss in a public forum—squicking is one of them.

SUBSUME

(1)   absorb; include; include within a larger class

(1) It has always been the practice of common-law judges to <u>subsume</u> local custom into their decision and judgments.

<u>Collocates to: differences, identity, individuals, knowledge, others</u>

TAKE A LESSON

(1)   learn from one's mistakes

TEMPORIZE

(1)   gain time by being evasive or indecisive

(2)   suit one's actions to the situation

(3)   parlay or deal so as to gain time

(4)   effect a compromise; negotiate

THROW SHADE

(1)   take a superior attitude; criticize, demean, or insult; diss or derogate

WOOLGATHER

(1)   appear to be lost in one's thoughts; daydream

BUSINESS AND EDUCATIONAL CONCEPTS

Branding, Advertising, Marketing, and Selling

ADVERTISE

(1)   amplify; brand; broadcast; communicate; disseminate; inform; market; notify; present; promote; publicize; recommend; sell

(2)   send paid communications through media channels to audiences who are most likely interested in the product, service, idea, or concept to which the advertising is referring

BENCHMARK

(1)   benchmark: learn from best practices; measure; point of references; standard; target

(1) "We still haven't played Madison Square Garden. That's a <u>bench-mark</u>. Something will have gone seriously wrong if we don't play Madison Square Garden for this album." —Dan Hawkins, English rock guitarist (1976–)

(1) "If your fund has trailed its <u>benchmark</u> for 12 months, three years, and five years, along with its peer group, then you have some pretty good reasons for selling." —Roy Weitz, founder of FundAlarm.com

Collocates to: assess, delivery, index, performance, rate, scores, success, set, test

BIRD DOG

(1) follow; watch and learn from an experienced person

BLAZON (blā'zən)

(1) advertise; proclaim something widely

COLLABORATE

(1) act as a team; assist; cooperate; pool resources; team up; work jointly with; work together

   (1) Dawn successfully <u>collaborated</u> with two other agencies.

CORRELATE

(1) associate with; calculate to show the reciprocal relation between; come together; bring into mutual relationship; correspond; parallel

Simile: "Care and labor are as much <u>correlated</u> to human existence as shadow is to light." —Harriet Beecher Stowe, American author (1811–1896); *Household Papers and Stories,* 1864, Part 2, Chapter 4

Collocates to: age, highly, moderately, negatively, positively, scores, significantly, with, variables

CROWD SOURCE

(1) identify a group with common demographics or psychographic characteristics and determine how to best make contact with it to deliver a message such as a sales or advertising message

E-TAIL

(1) online retail selling and business activities

CAPITALISM, FREE MARKETS, AND ENTREPRENEURSHIP

AFFILIATE

(1) associate; attach; belong to; combine; connect with; link; partner with; join

AMALGAMATE

(1) combine; fuse; integrate; join together; merge; mix; unite

BLUE SKY

(1) visionary thinking; out-of-the-box strategic, long-range thinking

   (1) I want to <u>blue sky</u> some ideas for new products for the youth market.

BOOTSTRAP

(1) have initiative; manage without assistance; succeed with few resources

   (1) The business founders <u>bootstrapped</u> their new start-up.

STOVE-PIPE

(1) develop, or be developed, in an isolated environment; solve narrow goals or meet specific needs in a way not readily compatible with other systems

   (1) "Apple had the sort of confusion present at most older organizations, where databases grew up with stove-piped or isolated islands of proprietary automation." —Sally Atkins, Open Systems Today, 20 September 1993

FINANCES AND MONEY

ASSET STRIP

(1) acquire a business or organization for the sole purpose of selling off its most valuable assets to make a quick profit

COLLATERALIZE

(1) pledge as collateral for financial consideration

CROWDFUND

(1) raise investment capital from multiple individuals online

(1) "Pebble Technologies Corporation, operating out of a cramped split-level condo, is racing to prove that it and the <u>crowdfunding</u> wave aren't flashes in the pan." —Pui Wing Tam, Wall Street Journal, *2 July 2012*

DISCOUNT

(1) convert future dollars (costs, investments, or revenue) into present values, accounting for interest costs or forgone investment income

ENGAGEMENT STACK

(1) chronologically ordered list of all the marketing touch points experienced by an individual user

(1) "You can imagine that, in many companies' marketing ecosystems, there can be millions of users and their individual <u>engagement stacks</u>." Phil Gross, Associate Director of Product Management at Visual IQ, The IQ Advisor, *issue 9, 12 September 2012*

ENUMERATE

(1) catalog; count off; itemize; list; tally

(2) determine the number of; total

(3) name one by one; specify

HYPOTHECATE

(1) pledge as security; mortgage

LEADERS, MANAGERS, SUPERVISORS

ADMINISTER

(1) control; deal out; direct; dispense; furnish a benefit; give out; govern; hand out; manage; mete out; order; run; supervise; oversee a process

AMALGAMATE (ə mal'gə māt')

(1) combine; fuse; integrate; join together; merge; mix; unite

ANALYZE

(1)   consider; dissect; evaluate; examine; explore; interpret; investigate; probe; question; scrutinize; study

(1) Randi analyzed the situation from all positions before making her decision.

APPROVE

(1)   accept; agree to; attest; back up; command; commend; endorse; favor; praise; ratify; sanction; support

(2)   allow; authorize; consent; grant; pass; sanction

ARRANGE

(1)   array; authorize; catalogue; classify; fix; order; organize; position; set up; make plans for something to be done

(1) Donna arranged for the managers to meet in the conference room.

ASSERT

(1)   affirm; allege; aver; avow; champion; claim; contend; declare; defend; emphasize; insist; maintain; protest; state strongly; stress; support claim of or for

(1) "The people know their rights, and they are never slow to assert and maintain them when they are invaded." —President Abraham Lincoln (1809–1865)

Parallelism: "Be daring, be different, be impractical, be anything that will assert integrity of purpose and imaginative vision against the play-it-safers, the creatures of the commonplace, the slaves of the ordinary." —Cecil Beaton, English photographer and fashion designer (1904–1980)

Collocates to: authority, control, claims, identity, independence, influence, interest, jurisdiction, leadership, privacy, privilege, rights

BATTEN

(1)   close; fasten; fix; secure

(2)   clean up; make large profits

BETA TEST

(1)   field test; sample prior to rollout; road-test

BLAMESTORMING

(1) sit in a group, discussing why things went wrong, why deadlines were missed, and so on, in an attempt to place blame on someone else

BLANDISH

(1) coax; cajole; influence; induce or persuade by gentle flattery

BRAINSTORM

(1) come up with; dream up; devise; freely generate ideas; think strategically; think

CONCEIVE

(1) create; envisage; imagine; invent original ideas; understand; picture; visualize

(2) elaborate; begin life; dream; form; make up

(1) "Four score and seven years ago, our fathers brought forth on this continent a new nation, <u>conceived</u> and dedicated to the proposition that all men are created equal." —President Abraham Lincoln

DASHBOARD

(1) monitor or gauge the statistics or status of a business; assessment

(1) "My company really only uses SPS for the document storage—not dashboarding, workflow, etc." —Michael Donahue, <u>Usenet: microsoft.public.sharepoint.portalserver</u>, 15 June 2002

DELIBERATE

(1) consider; contemplate; ponder; think about carefully

Metaphor: "Take time to <u>deliberate</u>, but when the time for action has arrived, stop thinking and go in." —Napoleon Bonaparte, French general and politician (1769–1821)

DESIGNATE

(1) call; circumscribe; choose; elect; entitle; identify; label; name; nominate; select; style; title

(2) allocate; indicate; point out; specify

DEVOLVE

(1) pass on rights and powers to another; pass powers to a deputy or successor

DISCERN

(1) behold; catch; descry; discriminate; distinguish; differentiate; have insight; make out; perceive; pick out; recognize; separate mentally from others; see things clearly; spot

EDUCE (ē doos')

(1) come to conclusion; solve a problem based on thoughtful consideration of facts; derive; evoke

(2) draw out; elicit; infer; deduce

(3) bring out or develop; elicit from

EFFECTUATE

(1) bring about; cause or accomplish something; effect

ENGENDER

(1) begat; bring about or into being; cause; create; give rise to; originate; produce

EXEMPLIFY

(1) illustrate by example; serve or show as a good example

INITIATE

(1) begin; create; commence; inaugurate; induct; install; instate; instigate; introduce; invest; kick off; open; set off; start

(1) Paula will be <u>initiating</u> a series of seminars on networking.

(2) coach; instruct; mentor; teach; train; tutor

INTERLARD

(1) intersperse; diversify; mix together

LEAN FORWARD

(1) be proactive; initiate a process or action

OPEN THE KIMONO

(1)   expose or reveal secrets or proprietary information

   (1) "Look, I will let you invest a million dollars in Apple if you will sort of open the kimono at Xerox PARC." —Steve Jobs

PERAMBULATE

(1)   walk through, over, and around to do a complete and thorough inspection

SHOTGUN

(1)   try a variety of methods; make repeated attempts; take an indiscriminate approach; be scattershot

ECONOMICS AND MONETARY

ACCRUE

(1)   accumulate; amass; ensue; build up; increase; mount up

   (1) After ten years, the investment accrued more interest that the original deposit.

(2)   come to one as a gain; amass

(3)   accrete; add; grow by addition

AMORTIZE

(1)   pay off (as a mortgage) gradually, usually by periodic payments of principal and interest

   (1) With larger payments, you should reduce debt so that the capital costs can be amortized over 20 years.

GAZUMP (gə'zŭmp)

(1)   raise the price of something, especially a house, after agreeing on a price verbally (with an intended buyer)

(2)   swindle or overcharge

PAINT THE TAPE

(1)   illegal action of stock market manipulators buying and/or selling a security among themselves to create artificial activity that, when reported on the ticker tape, would lure unexpected investors as they perceive unusual volume

(1)   "Tuesday's closing (stock) prices were particularly important to money managers who report their performances based upon quarterly figures, and suspicions of painting the tape." —Floyd Norris, New York Times, *10 January 2008*

QUANTIFY

(1)   Determine, express, or explain the quantity of; express something in numeric or quantifiable terms; to use a numerical expression or explanation

TAPE BOMB

(1)   report unexpected financial and economic news caused by a macro political event for the purpose of affecting stock and bond trading

(1)   "Wall Street Waits for the Next Tape Bomb" —Andrew Leonard, Wall Street Journal, *6 August 2007*

11

Education: Communications and Law

ACCOUTER (ə koot'ər)

(1) attire; clothe someone, especially for military purposes; equip with clothing; outfit

(1) The R.O.T.C. must accouter their cadets well in order to show off their candidates.

Simile: "Both accoutered like young men." —William Shakespeare, *Merchant of Venice* III:iv

ADDRESS

(1) deliver; direct; discourse; dispatch; direct one's attention to; forward; lecture; remark; speak directly to; talk to; mark with destination; refer to

(1) Juan addressed the class about the importance of teamwork.

(2) accost; adopt; attend to; come to; concentrate on; deal with; focus on; take up

Antithesis: "A man without an address is a vagabond; a man with two addresses is a libertine." —George Bernard Shaw, Irish playwright and essayist (1856–1950)

Alliteration: I am afraid you find my address will be more like an assault, and accost, that will agitate and aggravate the status quo.

Parallelism: "Lawyers are the implements of pain we set forth at one another. The first sent to address a situation, the retaliatory second to counterinflict and thereby equalize the pain imposed by the first. Repeat until both parties are economically depleted." —Unknown

Simile: "My <u>address</u> is *like* my shoes. It travels with me. I abide where there is a fight against wrong." —Mother Jones, American labor organizer (1830–1930)

AMPLIFY

(1)   augment; elevate; enlarge; expand; increase; intensify; magnify

   (1) "Most quarrels <u>amplify</u> a misunderstanding." —Andre Gide, French writer (1869–1951)

   (1) A hearing aid will <u>amplify</u> sound, not repair lost hearing.

(2)   add details to; clarify; develop; elaborate on; go into details about

ARRAY

(1)   align; gamut; lay out; set out for display or use; place in an orderly arrangement; regalia

(2)   place an order; marshal troops; parade

(3)   dress in fine or showy attire

Alliteration: "Days of <u>a</u>bsence, sad and dreary, Clothed in sorrow's dark <u>array</u>, Days of <u>a</u>bsence, I <u>a</u>m weary; She I love is far <u>a</u>way." —William Shakespeare, English dramatist, playwright, and poet (1564–1616)

Metaphor: "The schoolmaster is abroad! And I trust to him armed with his primer against the soldier in full military <u>array</u>." —Jeremy Bentham, English philosopher and activist (1748–1832)

Metaphor: "Stupidity, outrage, vanity, cruelty, iniquity, bad faith, falsehood/we fail to see the whole <u>array</u> when it is facing in the same direction as we." —Jean Rostand, French historian and biologist (1894–1977)

ARTICULATE

(1)   communicate; convey; be eloquent; enunciate; express; be fluent; formulate; be lucid; be a polemist; put into words; state; tell; verbalize

   (1) "Good business leaders create a vision, <u>articulate</u> the vision, passionately own the vision, and relentlessly drive it to completion." —Jack Welch, American chemical engineer, business executive, and author

Metaphor: "Talkers are usually more articulate than doers, since talk is their specialty." —Thomas Sowell, American writer and economist (1930–)

AUTHOR

(1) create; pen; scribe; source; write; compose; source of some form of intellectual or creative work

BANDY (ban'dē)

(1) exchange; give and receive

(1) His reputation has been bandied enough by his detractors.

(2) spread something in an unfavorable context

(3) toss or hit something back and forth

BLUE PENCIL

(1) correct or edit writing, as if by changing or deleting; cross out; censor

(1) The editors blue penciled some of the more descriptive dialog.

BLUE SKY

(1) employ visionary thinking; use out-of-the-box strategic, long-range thinking

BOOST

(1) advance; amplify; augment; encourage; enhance; further; heighten; hoist; improve; increase; lift; make better; raise

(1) "Outstanding leaders go out of their way to boost the self-esteem of their personnel. If people believe in themselves, it's amazing what they can accomplish." —Sam Walton, American businessman and entrepreneur (1918–1982)

CHAMPION

(1) advocate; back; campaign for; crusade for; excel; fight for; stand up for; support; uphold; be a winner

(1) "A champion is someone who gets up when he can't." —Jack Dempsey, former world heavyweight boxing champion

(1) "A champion is afraid of losing. Everyone else is afraid of winning." —Billy Jean King, tennis champion

Antithesis: "We cannot be both the world's leading champion of peace and the world's leading supplier of the weapons of war." —President Jimmy Carter

Repetition: "I am a member of a team, and I rely on the team, I defer to it and sacrifice for it, because the team, not the individual, is the ultimate <u>champion</u>." Mia Hamm, American soccer player (1972–)

CHRONICLE

(1)   account; diary; history; narrative; journal; record; register; story
Metaphor: "To <u>chronicle</u> the wars of kites and crows, fighting in the air." —John Milton, English poet, historian, and scholar (1608–1674)

Metaphor: "Life is easy to chronicle, but bewildering to practice." —E. M. Forster, English novelist and essayist (1879–1970)

COACH

(1)   advocate; back; campaign for; crusade for; excel; fight for; handler; manager; stand up for; support; tutor; uphold; be a winner
Simile: "Being in politics is *like* being a football <u>coach</u>. You have to be smart enough to understand the game and dumb enough to think it's important." —Eugene J. McCarthy, American democratic senator from Minnesota (1916)

COLLABORATE

(1)   act as a team; assist; cooperate; pool resources; team up; work jointly with; work together

(1) "In the long history of humankind (and animal kind, too) those who learned to <u>collaborate</u> and improvise most effectively have prevailed." —Charles Darwin, English naturalist (1809–1882)

Metaphor: "The purpose of life is to <u>collaborate</u> for a common cause; the problem is, nobody seems to know what it is." —Gerhard Gschwandtner, American businessman

COLLATE

(1)   assemble in proper sequence; bestow; compare critically; confer

(1) "To appreciate present conditions, <u>collate</u> them with those of antiquity." —Basil Bunting, British poet (1900–1985)

(1) <u>Collate</u> the results of the survey, and then begin to search for the distribution and dispersion of the data.

COLLOCATE

(1) have a strong tendency to occur side by side or be strongly associated with

(2) group, connect, or chunk together in a certain order; place close by one another

(1), (2) The students were asked to find synonyms that can <u>collocate</u> with certain words.

COMMUNICATE

(1) be in touch; connect; converse; correspond; convey something; exchange a few words; share; write

(1) I <u>communicated</u> the new pricing to all existing customers.

(1) "To effectively <u>communicate</u>, we must realize that we are all different in the way we perceive the world and use this understanding as a guide to our communication with others." —Tony Robbins, American self-help author and motivational speaker (1960–)

Antithesis: "The single biggest problem in <u>communication</u> is the illusion that it has taken place." —George Bernard Shaw, Irish literary critic, playwright, essayist, and winner of the 1925 Nobel Prize for Literature (1856–1950)

Metaphor: "Many attempts to <u>communicate</u> are nullified by saying too much." —Robert Greenleaf, American author and consultant

Parallelism: "He who knows, does not speak (<u>*communicate*</u>). He who speaks (<u>*communicates*</u>), does not know." —Lao Tzu, Chinese philosopher and founder of Taoism (600 B.C.–531 B.C.)

Repetition: "<u>Communicate</u>, <u>communicate</u>, and then <u>communicate</u> some more." —Bob Nelson, American stand-up comedian and actor (1958–)

Simile: "Good <u>communication</u> *is as* stimulating as black coffee, and just as hard to sleep after." —Anne Morrow Lindbergh, American writer and aviation pioneer (1906–2001)

Vivid imagery: "To listen well *is as* powerful a means of <u>communication</u> and influence *as to* talk well." —John Marshall, Supreme Court Justice of the United States (1755–1835)

CONCATENATE

(1) integrate; link together; unite or join in a series or chain

(2) combine two strings to form a single one

(1), (2) The <u>concatenate</u> function is a useful way to combine text from two or more fields into one field of a Microsoft Excel spreadsheet.

CONCEPTUALIZE

(1) conceive; create an understandable point out of a concept; make a concept of; interpret something from the abstract

Alliteration: It helps people to connect and conceive a complex idea such as creationism if you can conceptualize it.

CONCINNATE (kon-sŭh-nĕyt)

(1) arrange or blend skillfully; put together in a harmonious, precisely appropriate, or elegant manner; show skill and harmony, especially in a literary work; show an elegant arrangement

(1) A great manager has the ability to concinnate a diverse team with multiple skills and egos.

CONFABULATE

(1) chat, converse, or talk informally

(1) Jason confabulated about the trade expo for more than an hour.

CONJUGATE

(1) bring together; combine; contain two or more parts; couple; reciprocal; join; untied in pairs; yoked together

CORUSCATE

(1) brilliant in style; emit vivid flashes of light; flashy; showy; sparkle; scintillate

COUNSEL

(1) advise; advocate; deliberate; direct; guide; help; inform; mentor

(1) We will counsel our clients to be aware of Ponzi-type schemes.

(1) "I have only one counsel for you: Be master." —Napoleon Bonaparte, French general, politician, and emperor (1769–1821)

Metaphor: "When we turn to one another for counsel, we reduce the number of our enemies." —Khalil Gibran, Lebanese-born American philosophical essayist, novelist, and poet (1883–1931)

Metaphor: "Go not to the elves for counsel, for they will say both yes and no." —J. R. R. Tolkien, English writer and author of the epic fantasy *The Lord of the Rings* (1892–1973)

Parallelism: "He that gives good advice, builds with one hand; he that gives good <u>counsel</u> and example, builds with both; but he that gives good admonition and bad example, builds with one hand and pulls down with the other."
—Francis Bacon, Sr., English lawyer and philosopher (1561–1626)

Simile: "There is as much difference between the <u>counsel</u> that a friend giveth, and that a man giveth himself, as there is between the <u>counsel</u> of a friend and a flatterer." —Francis Bacon, Sr., English lawyer and philosopher

Vivid imagery: "There is a time to take <u>counsel</u> of your fears, and there is a time to never listen to any fear." Gen. George Patton, American general in World War I and World War II (1885–1945)

DEFINE

(1) characterize; classify; describe; determine, enumerate; make clear or set down boundaries; distinguish; explain or identify; label; name; state or set forth meaning of something; term

(1) circumscribe; delimitate; delimit; demarcate; mark out

(1), (2) Clearly <u>defining</u> the scope of the project will help prevent scope creep.

(1), (2) If it was before, it is no longer difficult to <u>define</u> a liberal and conservative voter.

Alliteration: If you can <u>d</u>escribe, <u>d</u>elineate, and <u>define</u> the <u>d</u>ifferences, you will have accomplished something no one thought was <u>d</u>oable.

DELEGATE

(1) allot; deputize; entrust; farm out; give; pass out; pass on authority; allocate; appoint; assign; authorize; choose; commit; depute; deputize; detail; elect; order; organize

(1) <u>Delegating</u> responsibilities to team members is one of the first tasks of a project manager.

(1) "Surround yourself with the best people you can find, <u>delegate</u> authority, and don't interfere." —President Ronald Reagan (1911–2004)

(1) "You can <u>delegate</u> authority, but not responsibility." —Stephen W. Comiskey

DELIMIT

(1) define; demarcate; determine; fix boundaries; restrict; set limits; state clearly

(1) An early step of research is to <u>delimit</u> the boundaries or what you will not attempt to do.

DELINEATE

(1)   describe accurately; determine; draw an outline; identify or indicate by marking with precision; fix boundaries; represent something

   (1) Philip's ideas about the new product were <u>delineated</u> in his proposal to the committee.

DISAMBIGUATE (dys am-big'yoo-āt')

(1)   establish a single grammatical or semantic interpretation for

EMIT (also see Earth and Nature)

(1)   express audibly

ENGAGE

(1)   engross; involve; occupy; participate; pledge; tie up; bind by a promise

   (1) "The primary vehicle that Pat uses to <u>engage</u> people is public speaking."

(2)   arrange for the services of; employ; hire

(3)   arrange for the use of; reserve

(4)   draw into; involve

(5)   attract and hold; employ and keep busy; occupy

(6)   mesh together

Repetition: "Certainly. Of course. That's PART of it. And always coming to school or when we're going home, you're to walk with me, when there ain't anybody looking—and you choose me and I choose you at parties, because that's the way you do when you're <u>engaged</u>." —Mark Twain, *Tom Sawyer*

Visual imagery: "'That is my own opinion,' replied the traveler; 'but one thing among many others seems to me very wrong in knights-errant, and that is that when they find themselves about to <u>engage</u> in some mighty and perilous adventure in which there is manifest danger of losing their lives, they never at the moment of engaging in it think of commending themselves to God, as is the duty of every good Christian in like peril; instead of which, they commend themselves to their ladies with as much devotion as if these were their gods, a thing which seems to me to savour somewhat of heathenism.'" Miguel Cervantes, *Don Quixote*

ESPOUSE (also see Religion, Ethics, and Morality)

(1) adopt; advocate; back; champion; promote; support; take up

(2) take as a wife

> *(1) The governor espoused a program of tax cuts.*

> *(2) "Effingham had, from the commencement of the disputes between the colonists and the crown, warmly maintained what he believed to be the just prerogatives of his prince; while, on the other hand, the clear head and independent mind of Temple had induced him to espouse the cause of the people." —James Fenimore Cooper,* The Pioneer

> *(2) "He should espouse Elizabeth her daughter." —William Shakespeare,* King Richard III

EVINCE

(1) reveal or indicate the presence of a particular feeling or condition; show plainly

(2) indicate; make manifest without a doubt

> *(1), (2) The final vote evinced every one of the Senator's true beliefs.*

> *(1), (2) "To judge from the conduct of the opposite parties, we shall be led to conclude that they will mutually hope to evince the justness of their opinions, and to increase the number of their converts by the loudness of their declamations and the bitterness of their invectives."*
> *—Alexander Hamilton, The Federalist Papers*

EXPATIATE (ek spā's/hē āt')

(1) elaborate; cover a wide scope of topics

> *(1) The professor's lecture expatiated beyond the printed syllabus.*

(2) add details to an account or an idea

(3) roam or wander freely

(4) speak or write in great detail

Alliteration: "Now, as the business of standing mast-heads, ashore or afloat, is a very ancient and interesting one, let us in some measure expatiate here."
—Herman Melville, *Moby Dick*

Vivid imagery: "When people are too well off, they always begin to long for something new. And so it came to pass, that the bird, while out one day, met a fellow bird, to whom he boastfully <u>expatiated</u> on the excellence of his household arrangements. But the other bird sneered at him for being a poor simpleton, who did all the hard work, while the other two stayed at home and had a good time of it. For, when the mouse had made the fire and fetched in the water, she could retire into her little room and rest until it was time to set the table. The sausage had only to watch the pot to see that the food was properly cooked, and when it was near dinner-time, he just threw himself into the broth, or rolled in and out among the vegetables three or four times, and there they were, buttered, and salted, and ready to be served. Then, when the bird came home and had laid aside his burden, they sat down to table, and when they had finished their meal, they could sleep their fill till the following morning: and that was really a very delightful life." —Grimm Brothers, *The Mouse, the Bird, and the Sausage*

EXPIATE (eks'pē āt')

(1) apologize; atone; make amends; make up; pay the penalty for; redress; suffer

Visual imagery: "But, in order to <u>expiate</u> the sin of avarice, which was my undoing, I oblige each passer-by to give me a blow." —Andrew Lang, *Arabian Nights*

Visual imagery: "Thou whose injustice hath supplied the cause That makes me quit the weary life I loathe, As by this wounded bosom thou canst see How willingly thy victim I become, Let not my death, if haply worth a tear, Cloud the clear heaven that dwells in thy bright eyes; I would not have thee <u>expiate</u> in aught The crime of having made my heart thy prey; But rather let thy laughter gaily ring And prove my death to be thy festival." —Miguel Cervantes, *Don Quixote*

EXPLICATE (eks'pli kāt')

(1) analyze logically; explain; make clear; write about something at great length

(1) The research findings will endeavor to <u>explicate</u> the theory of dark matter.

<u>Collocates to: cognition, findings, issues, orders, plans, social behavior, text</u>

EXPOSTULATE (ek späs'c/halāt')

(1) admonish; argue; complain; object; protest

(1) The generous nature of Safie was outraged by this command; she attempted to <u>expostulate</u> with her father, but he left her angrily, reiterating his tyrannical mandate. —Mary Shelley, Frankenstein

(2) reason with someone earnestly, objecting to that one's actions or intentions

EXTOL

(1) admire; exalt; glorify; laud; magnify; praise

FELICITATE (falis'i tāt')

(1) offer congratulations

FOMENT

(1) stir up public opinion; create a following based on dissent

GABBLE

(1) babble; talk rapidly and incoherently
Alliteration: "The discontented goose, who stoops to pass under the old gateway, twenty feet high, may <u>gabble</u> out, if we only knew it, a waddling preference for weather when the gateway casts its shadow on the ground." —Charles Dickens, *Bleak House*

GASCONADE

(1) show off; use extravagant, boastful talk

GESTICULATE (jes tik'yoo lāt')

(1) make exaggerated gestures when speaking

GIBBER (jib'ar)

(1) babble; balderdash; blatherskite; talk rapidly and incoherently
Repetition: "He ached with desire to express and could but <u>gibber</u> prosaically as everybody <u>gibbered</u>." —Jack London, *Martin Eden*

GRANDSTAND

(1) deliberate attempt to win applause from an audience

(1) In his political speech, the senator was accused by the press of *grandstanding* *when he made statements that were specifically designed to win quick applause from the audience but that did not contribute substantially to the matter under discussion.*

HEBETATE

(1) make something dull; make less responsive

IMBIBE (im bīb')

(1) soak in or up; steep; take in; receive in the mind and retain

(1) In the 20 years I have known him, I have never seen him *imbibe* *that much liquor.*

INCULCATE

(1) impress a belief or idea on someone by repeating it until the idea is accepted

(1) "When schools fail to *inculcate* *American values, giving short shrift to the history of the American Revolution, the American Civil War, and the American Civil Rights Movement, while emphasizing the history of Africa, Latin America, or Asia, they are severing the ties that bind Americans together in the name of diversity." —Jennifer Braceras, "Not Necessarily in Conflict: Americans Can Be Both United and Culturally Diverse,"* Harvard Journal of Law & Public Policy *29, issue 1, Fall 2005, p. 27–32*

(2) teach by persistent urging

(3) implant ideas through constant admonishing

INTERPOLATE

(1) introduce something often unnecessary; insert; interpose; intercalate; incorporate; include; introduce; throw in

Antithesis: "'You're a thousand times better than me—' he attempted to interpolate, but was in turn interrupted." —Jack London, *Burning Daylight*

INVOCATE

(1)   speak at an invocation

JUXTAPOSE

(1)   adjoin; place side by side or close together for purposes of comparison; put side by side to compare

(1) "Although a number of journalists and academicians have alluded in passing to similarities between Jimmy Carter and Bill Clinton, no systematic attempt has been made to juxtapose their presidencies." —Phillip Henderson, *"Clinton, Carter, and the Policy Wonk Presidency,"* Perspectives on Political Science *26, issue 3, Summer 1997, p. 149*

LIAISE (lē āz')

(1)   establish a liaison with
Repetition: "I am simply a liaison. I liaise." —Dylan, *The Transformers: Dark of the Moon*

NATTER

(1)   babble or talk ceaselessly; blather; chatter; chitchat; have a chat; gossip; grumble; jaw; talk
Alliteration: "In the United States today, we have more than our share of the nattering nabobs of negativism." —Vice President Spiro Agnew

PERSEVERATE

(1)   continue something; repeat something insistently

PONTIFICATE

(1)   express opinions in a pompous and dogmatic way; blowhard

PRATE (prāt)

(1)   babble; blather; chatter in a childish way; gibber; jabber; prattle; rant; talk foolishly or at tedious length

(1) "In the present system of the National Institute of Health grants, there is no way to succeed. No matter how much they prate in public about thinking outside the box and rewarding 'high-risk' proposals, the reviewers are the same and their self-interest is the same." —Tom Bethell, "Challenging Conventional Wisdom," American Spectator *38, issue 6, p. 50–53*

Alliteration: "All periods prate against one another in your spirits; and the dreams and pratings of all periods were even realer than your awakeness!" —Friedrich Nietzsche, German philosopher (1844–1900)

Metaphor: "This I conceive to be no time to prate of moral influences. Our men's nerves require their accustomed narcotics and a glass of whiskey is a powerful friend in a sunstroke, and these poor fellows fall senseless on their heavy drills." —Clara Barton, founder of the American Red Cross (1821–1912)

PRATTLE

(1)   chat; gab incoherently or indistinctly; jabber; talk rapidly; talk nonsense

(1) "Every young man who came to the house—seeing those impressionable, smiling young faces (smiling probably at their own happiness), feeling the eager bustle around him, and hearing the fitful bursts of song and music and the inconsequent but friendly prattle of young girls ready for anything and full of hope—experienced the same feeling; sharing with the young folk of the Rostovs' household a readiness to fall in love and an expectation of happiness." —Leo Tolstoy, Russian writer (1828–1910)

RETORT

(1)   answer in kind; reply in a sharp, retaliatory manner; say in reply or response in kind

SEGUE (seg'wā)

(1)   continue without break; lead into new areas; proceed without interruption; smoothly change to the next topic

(1) Drew segued nicely from the previous speaker's closing remarks into his Nobel Prize acceptance speech.

STYLEFLEX

(1)   deliberately attempt to adjust one's communication style to accommodate others

SUBTILIZE

(1)   mark fine distinctions and subtleties; make senses more keen; make more subtle or refined

SYMBOLIZE

(1)   express indirectly by an image, form, or model

> *(1) "We observe today not a victory of party, but a celebration of free-dom—symbolizing an end, as well as a beginning—signifying renewal, as well as change." —President John F. Kennedy, inaugural address, 20 January 1961*

(2)   represent or identify by using a symbol

Repetition: "But we cannot symbolize the fact that Plato does not precede Socrates by not putting the word 'precedes' between 'Plato' and 'Socrates.'" —Bertrand Russell, British philosopher, logician, mathematician, and historian (1872–1970)

X OUT

(1)   eliminate; mark out

LAW

ABDUCE (also see Art)

(1)   advance evidence for; allege; cite

ACQUIT

(1)   clear; exculpate; discharge completely; exonerate; find not guilty

(2)   release from duty

Antithesis: "Knightley had once told her it was because she saw in her the really accomplished young woman, which she wanted to be thought herself; and though the accusation had been eagerly refuted at the time, there were moments of self-examination in which her conscience could not quite acquit her." —Jane Austen, English novelist (1775–1817)

ADJUDICATE (əjoo-'di kāt')

(1)   act as judge; listen; mediate; preside over an argument; settle

> *(1) Susan tried her best to adjudicate the dispute as the sales team argued back and forth over the commission plan.*

Alliteration: "He was the man with power to buy, to build, to choose, to endow, to sit on committees and adjudicate upon designs, to make his own terms for placing anything on a sound business footing." —George Bernard Shaw, Irish playwright and cofounder of the London School of Economics (1856–1950)

ADVOCATE

(1) advance; back; be in favor of; bolster; defend; encourage; promote; sponsor; support

Repetition: "It's not really that I've been an <u>advocate</u> for hearing aids for a long time; it's just that I've been losing my hearing for a long time! So it's actually very important for me because I'm actually hearing impaired and I simply want to hear better!" —Leslie Nielsen, American actor and comedian (1926–2010)

AMERCE

(1) fine; punish

ARRAIGN

(1) accuse of a wrong or inadequacy; be called before a court in a criminal case during which the defendant is informed of his or her rights and is required to plead guilty or not guilty

Simile: "The history of reform is always identical; it is the comparison of the idea with the fact. Our modes of living are not agreeable to our imagination. We suspect they are unworthy. We <u>arraign</u> our daily employments." —Ralph Waldo Emerson

CEDE

(1) abandon; abdicate; admit; assign; concede; give or hand over; give up; grant; let go; relinquish; render; surrender; transfer; yield

(1) He <u>ceded</u> the land to the city for a public park.

Parallelism: "And nobility will not be able to help you with your love; Love does not know how to <u>cede</u> to ancestral images." —Propertius Sextus

CIRCUMVALLATE

(1) surround with or use as a rampart or fortification

CONCILIATE

(1) appease; gain the regard or good or goodwill by good acts; pacify; reconcile; soothe the anger of; win over

(1) All parties will be provided an opportunity to <u>conciliate</u> or resolve the matter during the course of the investigation.

Alliteration: "As it was, she constantly doubted her own conclusions, because she felt her own ignorance: how could she be confident that one-roomed cottages were not for the glory of God, when men who knew the classics appeared to conciliate indifference to the cottages with zeal for the glory?" —George Eliot, pen name of Mary Ann Evans, English novelist (1819–1880)

CONTRAVENE

(1) be in breach of; breach; break; contradict; deny; disobey; disregard; flout; violate

Parallelism: "Nature is always consistent, though she feigns to contravene her own laws." —Ralph Waldo Emerson

DEPONE

(1) declare under oath; give evidence; make a deposition; testify

(1) "These two females did afterwards depone that Mr. Willet in his consternation uttered but one word, and called that up the stairs in a stentorian voice, six distinct times." —Charles Dickens, English writer and social critic (1812–1870)

EXCULPATE

(1) absolve; clear; declare or prove guiltless; discharge; dispense; exempt; free from blame; let off; pardon; relieve; spare

(1) "The unblushing Macdonald, without even endeavouring to exculpate himself from the crime he was charged with, meanly endeavoured to reproach Sophia with ignobly defrauding him of his money." —Jane Austen, English novelist (1775–1817)

EXONERATE

(1) absolve; acquit; clear; forgive; pardon; vindicate

(1) Justin spent 15 years in prison before new DNA evidence helped exonerate him.

(1) "'I imagine one cannot exonerate such a man from blame, though he is your brother,' said Alexey Alexandrovitch severely." —Leo Tolstoy, Russian writer (1828–1910)

EXPROPRIATE

(1)   take something without owner's consent

(2)   deprive of ownership; dispossess

(1) Unfortunately, the federal law of imminent domain is too often used by local governments to <u>expropriate</u> land that could not be purchased otherwise.

Alliteration: "Under current choice-of-law rules, each State has an incentive to <u>expropriate</u> out-of-state corporations to benefit in-state plaintiffs." — Michele Greve, "Business, the States, and Federalism's Political Economy," *Harvard Journal of Law & Public Policy* Summer 2002, Vol. 25 Issue 3, p895

Parallelism: "<u>Expropriate</u> the capitalists through the state which the capitalists created." —Unknown

EXPUNGE

(1)   blot out; cancel; cut; delete; erase completely; wipe out

(1) The district attorney made the deal <u>expunging</u> his criminal record in exchange for his testimony in another case.

EXPURGATE (eks'pər gāt')

(1)   seize property from its owner for public sale

(2)   remove passages from works deemed obscene

(3)   delete; expunge

INCULPATE

(1)   incriminate, blame, or charge with a crime

(1) With current DNA technology available for criminal cases, it will either <u>inculpate</u> or exculpate the guilty or the innocent.

INURE

(1)   accept what is not due or earned

(1) In a disturbing trend lately, presidents of nonprofit organizations have been <u>inuring</u> payoffs from vendors of the organization.

(1) "Often privatization is motivated by profit, and that doesn't <u>inure</u> to the public benefit as often as we'd like." —David Patterson, former New York governor

SEQUESTER

(1)   isolate a portion from the larger population

(2)   confiscate; seize; take over

Parallelism: "Let him <u>sequester</u> himself, from the company of his countrymen, and diet in such places, where there is good company of the nation where he travelleth." —Sir Francis Bacon, English author, courtier, and philosopher (1561–1626)

12

Technology: Control, Fields of Technology, Measurement, Science, Tools, and Machines

AMAZON RANK

(1) censor to exclude content

CHIMP

(1) take a digital photo and look at it on the camera's screen

(1) "With film there's no comparable chimp factor unless you're taking pictures with something like a Polaroid camera." —Usenet rec.photo. digital group (http://groups.google.com/group/rec.photo.digital/msg/ a16c97e98f49e407?dmode=source&hl=en)

CLICKSTREAM

(1) count and observe consumer behavior on Web sites

(1) The digital strategy included plans to clickstream the visitor data to the Web site.

COLD-IRON

(1) receive electricity, heat, water, and other utilities on a ship or boat from shore side

(1) "The state of Alaska has imposed emission regulations in respect of soot, with quite severe penalties if exceeded, and several harbors in Sweden require cold-ironing or emission reductions when some of the larger ferries are in port." —Lloyd's List International, 23 September 1993

CONFLATE

(1) combine or mix two different elements

COROTATE

(1) rotate with, or at the same time or rate as, another body

CYBERHOARD

(1) accumulate a pointless and excessive number of photos and Word documents on one's hard drive

CYBERNATE

(1) control a function, process, or creation by a computer

DEBUG

(1) clear up; correct; eliminate errors or malfunctions; fix; mend; repair; restore; service; sort out

DEVOLATILIZE

(1) make or become free of volatile matter

E-SOURCE

(1) processes and use of tools that electronically allow all activities in the digital sourcing process

GEOCAST

(1) participate in a high-tech treasure-hunting game played throughout the world by adventure seekers equipped with GPS devices

GOOGLE BOMB

(1) use a script to search via Google for a word or phrase millions of times, making it appear as if many different people actually searched for it; to conspire with other web page authors to create a Google bomb by agreeing on the search phrase and victim site

GOOGLE DANCE

(1) index update of the Google search engine

MORPH (also see the Earth and Nature)

(1)   change shape and form in a computer animation

(2)   change shape in form

(2)   *"Kate Moss is an equivalent cultural icon, a kind of living Barbie for the '90s. It's her ability to <u>morph</u> into so many different characters with minor changes in makeup and hair (courtesy of makeup master Dick Page and hair pro Nicholas Jurnjack), her capacity to transform herself over and over, that keeps us captivated." —Susan Vaughan, "Transformer," Bazaar, issue 3,454, September 1999, p. 464*

SMOG

(1)   smog check; to certify that a vehicle meets emission standards

ZOT (slang)

(1)   in slang usage on the Internet, to remove, censor, or ban material or participants

(2)   strike or destroy, especially with lightning or other beam or jolt of energy

Sources

Barker, John, *400 Words You Should Know* (New York: Houghton Mifflin Harcourt Publishing Co., 2010), Chapter 12.

Beyer, Thomas, Jr., Ph.D., *501 English Verbs,* 2nd edition (New York: Baron's Educational Series, 2007).

Bly, Robert, *The Words You Should Know to Sound Smart* (Avon, Mass.: Adams Media, 2009).

Crystal, David, *The Cambridge Encyclopedia of the English Language* (Cambridge, Mass.: Cambridge University Press, 1995).

Davies, Mark, The Corpus of Contemporary American English (COCA), *450 Million Words, 1990–Present* (1998). Available online at http://corpus.byu.edu/coca/.

Dictionary by Hampton, application on iPhone.

Fenell, Barbara, A., *A History of the English Language* (Oxford: Blackwell Publishers, 2001).

Kellen, Kim, *Career Planning, A Development Approach* (Upper Saddle River, N.J.: Merrill, 1998).

Lucas, Stephen, *The Art of Public Speaking,* 9th edition (Boston: McGraw-Hill, 1983).

Montefiore, Simon Sebag, *Speeches That Changed the World* (London: Quercus Publishing, 2005).

Noonan, Peggy, *To-Do List: A Sentence, Not 10 Paragraphs, Wall Street Journal* Opinion, 26 June 2009.

Orwell, George, "Politics and The English Language," at http://georgeorwellnovels.com/essays/notes-for-politics-and-the-english-language/. Accessed 20–24 October 2012.

Roget's II The New Thesaurus, The American Heritage Dictionary (Boston: Houghton Mifflin Co., 1980).

Sisson, A. R., *Sisson's Word and Expression Locator* (West Nyak, N.Y.: Parker Publishing Co., 1979).

Wilfred, Funk, Dr., and Norman Lewis, *30 Days to a More Powerful Vocabulary* (New York: Simon & Shuster, 1942).

www.rfp-templates.com/List-of-Action-Verbs.html. Accessed
  2–12 August 2008.

www.writeexpress.com/action-verbs.html. Accessed 2–12 August
  2008.

Index

*Words in **bold** are power verbs.

B

indurate, 103
initiate, 119
interlard, 119
interpolate, 134
interpose, 78, 111
intervene, 54
intransitive verbs, 15
intuit, 111
inure, 140
inveigle, 78
investing, buying versus, 6
invocate, 135

J–K

jawbone, 54
Johnson, Lyndon B., 5
journal, 34
jump ugly, 79
juxtapose, 135

Keaton, Diane, 3
Kennedy, John F., 3
king, 33
Kipling, Rudyard, 1
knock and drag, 54

L

language. *See also* body language; words
    competence versus
        performance in, 10
    inconsistency of English
        rules, 9-10
    learning process for, 4
    phrasing of, 19-20
    power of, 4-6
    pronunciation, 13
launch, 61

law verbs, 137-141
lean forward, 119
liaise, 135
lightning, 9
limn, 30
Lincoln, Abraham, 3, 5
lindy bomb, 31
linguistics, goal of, 10
Locke, John, 5
lour, 79
Luce, Clare Booth, 3
Luntz, Frank, 2, 7
lustrate, 103

M

macerate, 64
machinate, 79
mail it in, 30
make (one's) bones, 79
maledict, 103
management verbs, 116-120
marketing verbs, 113-114
mash up, 33
maze, 79
medicine verbs, 63-64
meliorate, 92, 103
merk, 79
metamorphose, 40
metaphor, defined, 19
mete, 111
mew, 111
military verbs, 56-62
militate, 103
mission, defined, 7
mitigate, 40
mollify, 92
mollycoddle, 92
morality verbs, 97-104

FT Press

FINANCIAL TIMES

In an increasingly competitive world, it is quality
of thinking that gives an edge—an idea that opens new
doors, a technique that solves a problem, or an insight
that simply helps make sense of it all.

We work with leading authors in the various arenas
of business and finance to bring cutting-edge thinking
and best-learning practices to a global market.

It is our goal to create world-class print publications
and electronic products that give readers
knowledge and understanding that can then be
applied, whether studying or at work.

To find out more about our business
products, you can visit us at www.ftpress.com.